Writing
Strategies

Writing Strategies

A STUDENT-CENTERED APPROACH
BOOK ONE: INTERMEDIATE

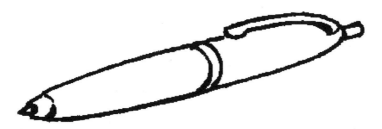

**David Kehe
and Peggy Dustin Kehe**

PRO LINGUA ASSOCIATES

Pro Lingua Associates, Publishers

P.O. Box 1348
Brattleboro, Vermont 05302-1348 USA
Office: 802 257 7779
Orders: 800 366 4775
Email: info@ProLinguaAssociates.com
      orders@ProLinguaAssociates.com
SAN: 216-0579
Webstore: www.ProLinguaAssociates.com

At ***Pro Lingua***
our objective is to foster an approach
to learning and teaching that we call
interplay, *the **inter**action of language*
learners and teachers with their materials,
with the language and culture,
and with each other in active, creative
*and productive **play**.*

ISBN 0-86647-161-8

Writing Strategies was designed by Arthur A. Burrows. It was set in Adobe Times, a digital font based on Times New Roman, at present one of the most popular type faces. Being consistent in weight and color, with sharp neoclassical serifs, it is easy to read even when set small or printed badly. Its bold is bold and italic legible. Times New Roman is an early Twentieth Century type developed either by Victor Lardent in London in 1931 or by Starling Burgess in the United States in 1904 – there is historical controversy. No matter who drew the original Times New Roman, it was drawn from classical Roman fonts initially popular in the 1700's because they adapted well for setting Greek. The same characteristics have made it the most common modern type for phonetic alphabets and multilingual texts. This book was printed and bound by Capital City Press of Montpelier, Vermont.

The reading selections used in *Section 2: Fluency Writing* have been rewritten for this book but are based on articles from the following sources: ***A Boy is Burned:*** "Boy Burned Trying TV Fire Stunt with Friends." *Seattle Post-Intelligencer, September 19, 1997.* ***Grizzly Bears:*** "Grizzly-Bear Attacks: Get Used to Them." *Seattle Times, August 18, 1996.* ***Cheating at School:*** "Classroom Cheating." *Stevens Point (WI) Journal, April 28, 1990.* ***Police Dogs:*** "Canines with a Dogged Love for Police Work." *Seattle Post-Intelligencer, August 28, 1998.* And "Amid Dangers of Duty, Police Dog is Often an Officer's Best Friend." *Seattle Post-Intelligencer,* January 1, 2000. ***Music Therapy:*** "I Know It's Only Music Therapy, But I Like It." *The Hartford Courant* (reprinted in *The Japan Times, June 30, 1996).* ***Stopping a Drunk Driver:*** "Alcohol-Sensing Lock May Become Law." *Seattle Post-Intelligencer, February 27, 1998.* ***Sleep for Students:*** "Schools Start Too Early, Experts Say." *Seattle Post-Intelligencer, August 26, 1996.* ***Unattractive Men:*** "Competition Gets Ugly for Fair-of-Face Males." *The Japan Times* (date unknown).

Printed in the United States of America
First printing 2003. 1000 copies.

Contents

CONTENTS

SECTION 2: FLUENCY WRITING

CONTENTS

SECTION 3: GRAMMAR EXERCISES

CONTENTS

User's Guide

Writing Strategies
A Student-Centered Approach

Book One

Introduction

The purpose of this book and its companion volume is to help ESL students at the pre-college, community college, and college level meet the requirements of academic and professional writing. There is sufficient material in the two books for two semesters of work.

The texts are the source material for implementing a course in which teachers have ample time to work individually with students. As the term "student-centered" in the sub-title implies, the students spend most of their class time at work on their writing skills. They learn to develop the skills of writing by writing, not listening to the teacher, or reading long explanations.

There are three sections in each of the two books. Each section features a different aspect of writing skills development. The sections are Rhetorical Modes, Fluency Writing, and Grammar.

▬▬▬ SECTION 1: MODES ▬▬▬

Rhetorical Modes are the focus of the first and basic section of each book. Most writing skills texts focus on these modes. Those covered in the two books are:

Book One	Book Two
Description	Process
Narration	Cause and Effect
Exposition	Extended Definition
Comparison and Contrast	Argumentation

SECTION 2: FLUENCY WRITING

The **Fluency Writing** section engages the students in a structured alternative to free writing or journal writing. Each activity involves pairs or triads of students in cooperative speaking, listening, and reading work with an article about real-world topics. In the final step of each activity, the students write paragraphs with the details of the article without looking at it. This requires them to make active use of the new vocabulary and sentence styles they have just worked with.

SECTION 3: GRAMMAR

The **Grammar** section is a series of activities that focus on grammatical terminology and grammatical problems typically encountered by intermediate and advanced level students as they develop their skill in accurate and proficient compositions. There are two types of activities — one type involves the students working individually on a grammar problem. The other involves groups of three students working together on the problem.

The three sections can be used in a variety of ways, but a recommended procedure is to use the Rhetorical Modes section as the basis, proceeding step-by-step through the eight modes. The Fluency Writing is done at any time during the course when there is a natural break during the work on the Rhetorical Modes. The Grammar activities can also be done at any time when it is apparent that it is needed, although there are suggestions throughout the Rhetorical Modes section for using these activities.

Used together, the three sections of the book provide challenge and variety to the students while allowing the teacher time to work one-on-one with the students.

Writing Strategies

Section 1: Modes

Mode 1: Description ·

Mode 2: Narration ·

Mode 3: Exposition ·

Mode 4: Comparison and Contrast Essay ·

Mode 1: Description

(Descriptive essays describe something such as a scene, a person, a thing, a feeling, etc.)

Fluency Writing: Before starting this unit, do a Fluency Writing from Section 2, pages 112-139. After finishing, begin working individually on the following exercises.

Essay 1: *Describing a Scene*
Part 1: *Focusing on the unique features*

Expressions

> ### *Expressions for describing a scene*
>
> | | | | |
> |---|---|---|---|
> | • at the top | • in front of | • outside | • on the left |
> | • above | • beside | • inside | • in the middle/center |
> | • next to | • beyond | • behind | • on the right |
> | • below/under | • in the distance | • nearest to | • near |
> | • at the bottom | • in the back | • farthest from | |

Exercise 1: Underline the expressions for describing a scene.

My father's desk has some important things on it. <u>On the right side</u>, there is a black telephone. Next to the phone is a picture of my family that was taken during our vacation. In the middle of the desk is his computer. My father spends a lot of time at this desk every day talking on the phone and using his computer.

Yesterday, Fred couldn't park his car in his garage because it was full of things. In the middle of the garage was his son's bike. Behind the bike, there were some boxes of old clothes that his wife wanted to give away. In the left corner stood a ladder with a hose beside it. After moving all of these things, Fred could finally park his car in the garage.

At the entrance to the city zoo, there is a lot of activity. Nearest to the entrance, a man in a bright blue booth sells peanuts that we can feed to the animals. Beyond the peanut seller, we can see a hill surrounded by trees with monkeys running and jumping. Outside the monkey area, there is a group of children holding colorful balloons, watching the monkeys and laughing. It's always a lot of fun to come to the zoo and see all the action.

Sample essay, first draft

Exercise 1: Fill in the blanks in the essay, "A Visit to the Countryside," with the correct words from the box. As you use a word, check it off in the box, as we have with the word "countryside."

• view __	• enjoyable __	• countryside **✗**	• mountains __
• in front of __	• realize __	• excitement __	

Introduction to the scene

A Visit to the Countryside

The other day, I was invited to visit my friend who lives in the ___*countryside*___. Before going, I was not excited about leaving the _____ of the city, where I live, because I thought the countryside would be boring. After I arrived, we ate lunch. Her table was placed _____ a big window, so, during the lunch, we were able to look outside. My friend's house is located on top of a hill, so we could see a great _____ while eating. The scene looked like this.

View of the scene

Conclusion: Explanation of why this was important/memorable/special

In conclusion, my day in the countryside turned out to be surprisingly _____. I knew the countryside would be beautiful with _____, forests and open spaces. However, I did not _____ that there could be so many things to do, like skiing, horseback riding, swimming, and even seeing ghosts.

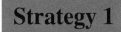 **Strategy 1** Draw a picture of the scene before describing it.

Exercise 1:

❶. Choose a scene from below.

❷. Draw a picture of your scene.

Possible scenes

- a photo of you as a child on vacation
- your childhood neighborhood
- your apartment or dorm room or home
- a music concert
- a view from an airplane window
- a view from your bedroom window/ a classroom window/ a car window
- a postcard
- other view: tell your teacher about your idea before drawing

---

Grammar: *For practice with* **Subjects** *and* **Verbs**, *do Grammar Unit 1 in Section 3.*

Strategy 2 Write a good introduction.

Writing a Good Introduction to a Scene

A good introduction gives some background information about the scene.
It does not begin describing the objects in the scene.

Exercise 1:
  ❶. Write **Good** next to the *three introductions* that tell background information.
  ❷. Write **Weak** next to the *two introductions* that describe objects/people in a scene.

_____ *Introduction 1*

My grandmother's house was the place which we always visited during the holidays.
At the beginning of the holiday season, she spent hours and hours preparing food
and decorating her house, especially the living room, where we spent most of the
day.

_____ *Introduction 2*

For his job, my father travels a lot. When I was ten years old, he took me with him
on a business trip to Africa. I have a picture that someone took of us in a busy
market place in one of the cities that we visited.

_____ *Introduction 3*

In front of the café were two small tables with four chairs around them. Nobody
was sitting at the tables yet because it was too early in the morning. A waiter,
wearing a white apron, was sweeping the sidewalk around the tables with a broom.
He looked very sleepy.

_____ *Introduction 4*

A terrible tornado hit our town last spring. Fortunately nobody was hurt, but there
was a lot of damage. After the weather cleared, I took a walk through the
neighborhood that was hit the worst by the tornado.

_____ *Introduction 5*

On the right side of the scene, there were two people, a man and a woman, standing
next to a large painting. The painting looked like modern art, and the two people
seemed to be trying to understand it. On the left side of this scene, I could see a
group of five people gathered around one person. They seemed to be a group of
tourists listening to their tour leader describe the museum.

Strategy 3   Write a good conclusion.

> ### Writing a Good Conclusion to a Scene
>
> A **good** conclusion explains why the scene was important, memorable or special for you. It does not include a description of objects or people.

Exercise 1:
  ❶. Write **Good** next to the *three conclusions* that tell background information.
  ❷. Write **Weak** next to the *two conclusions* that describe objects/people in a scene.

_____ *Conclusion 1*

It looked like the children were almost finished building their snow man. He was about five feet tall. His eyes were two black stones, and his mouth was made from five black ones. His nose was a carrot. There was no hat, but he had a scarf around his neck.

_____ *Conclusion 2*

Although many people laugh when I show them that picture of my first grade classroom, I feel attached to it. Everything in this room was new for me, so there was so much for me to learn. After the year I spent in that classroom, I felt like I was no longer a little child anymore.

_____ *Conclusion 3*

Behind my friends was a huge pine tree. In fact, it was so large that some park workers made a hole through the middle of its base so that cars could drive through. Next to the tree was a sign giving some information about the age and height of the tree.

_____ *Conclusion 4*

I have mixed emotions about that gym. On the one hand, I feel good about it because I was able to recover from my back injury by getting exercise there. On the other hand, the gym reminds me of the many hours of painful workouts and sweat.

_____ *Conclusion 5*

During that week that I visited my friend, I lived like a queen. Unless I become a millionaire someday, I'm sure that I will never again stay in such a beautiful house. I will especially remember that room with the gigantic fireplace and sofa because of the evenings we spent looking at the fire and talking about our dreams for the future.

Grammar: *For practice with* **Conjunctions,** *do Grammar Unit 2 in Section 3.*

Strategy 4 Write an introduction and conclusion before describing the scene.

Exercise 1:
- ❶. Write an introduction that gives some background information about the scene which you drew on page 5.
- ❷. Write a conclusion that explains why this scene was important, memorable, or special to you.

_____

_____

_____

_____

_____

_____

_____

_____

Do not write the middle paragraph describing the scene.

_____

_____

_____

_____

_____

Strategy 5 Write a first draft with some details.

Exercise 1:

❶. Look at the scene of the countryside illustrating "A Visit to the Countryside" on page 4.

❷. Fill in the blanks with phrases from the box to complete the first-draft of the main paragraph describing of scene. As you use a phrase, check it off in the box, as we have with the phrase "At the top of the mounain."

(**Notice:** This is a first draft, so it is short and simple, and it may have some grammar mistakes.)

> - In the middle of the scene ___
> - on top of the hill on the right ___
> - On the left side ___
> - At the top of the mountain _**X**_
> - In front of the trees and on the left ___
> - Just below the lodge ___

_____, there was a small mountain, where

people go skiing in winter. _____*At the top of the mountain,*_____ there was a ski lodge.

_____, I could see a skier. At the bottom of the mountain

was a forest of pine and oak trees. _____

_____, I could see a small house. _____ there was

a man with a horse. Also, there was a road going from the middle in the front to the upper

right side. The road was going to a big house, which was located _____

_____. It was a

sunny day with white clouds and a blue sky. It looked beautiful!

Exercise 2: Write a first-draft description of the scene that you drew on page 5.

Grammar Groups: *For practice with* **Subjects, Verbs,** *and* **Conjunctions,**
do Grammar Unit 3 in Section 3.

Essay 1: *Describing a Scene* • **Part 2:** *Preparing to write the first draft* • **9**

Part 3: *Writing the second draft*

(Think about your second draft while you do the exercises in this part.)

Strategy 6 Add details to the description of objects.

Exercise 1: Fill in the blanks with the correct words from the box.

- It looked like someone had hit it with a car. __
- which kept my feet warm when I got up on winter mornings. __
- This type of sauce would probably be good on Chinese or Mexican food. __
- which was messy and covered with papers. __
- His name was Coco because he was the color of chocolate. __

In the right corner was my desk, _____

_____

Next to the garage, there was a garbage can with a dent in the side. _____

_____

_____

My dog always slept to the right of the sofa. _____

_____

Next to my bed was a large round gray rug, _____

_____

On the table, there was a bottle of hot sauce. _____

_____

Exercise 2: Choose three of these topics and write extra details, like those in Exercise 1.

1. The car was old and broken down.

2. The restaurant was at the top of a tall building.

3. We could see a boat on the lake.

4. Next to the barn, there was a pig.

5. My best friend was sitting on a bench.

6. At the parade . . .

7. *(Your choice)*

Strategy 7 Add details to the description of people.

Exercise 1: Fill in the blanks with the correct words from the box.

> - hair __ • sisters __ • asleep __ • looked like **X**
> - wet __ • dolls __ • skin __

1. On the beach, a man was lying on the sand. It _**looked like**_ he had been there a long time because his face was very red from the sun. He must have fallen _____ there.

2. A teenager was standing near the waterfalls. His _____ and clothes were soaking _____ because he had stood under the falls.

3. Two small girls were playing with _____ on the front step of the house. I'm sure that they were _____ because they looked alike. They were talking to each other through their dolls.

> - was pointing __ • bottle __ • movie __
> - looked __ • crying __ • magazine __

4. There was a mother holding a baby. She _____ tired from carrying the heavy child, who was _____. The mother was trying to put a _____ in his mouth.

5. In front of the magazine rack, two girls, who were about 16 years old, were looking at a _____. One of the girls _____ at something, and the other one was laughing. I think that the magazine was about _____ stars.

Exercise 2: Choose three of the topics below and write extra details like those in Exercise 1.

1. A boy was sitting in front of the computer.
2. In the back row of the theater, a young couple was sitting.
3. There were two boys running . . .
4. In the front seat of the car, I could see . . .
5. Standing next to the policeman was an old lady . . .
6. A very tall man was talking to the clerk.
7. *(Your choice)*

Write a second draft and add details.

Exercise 1: Fill in the blanks in the essay below, "A Visit to the Countryside," with the correct phrases from the box. As you use a phrase, check it off in the box, as we have with the word "My friend said..." ***Notice:** This is the second draft of the sample essay you started on page 4.*

- My friend told me that in summer he often jogged up to that house and swam in the pool there. __
- My friend said that it was the second highest mountain in the state. ✗
- place for tourists __
- I was not sure what he was doing, but perhaps he was training the horse for a show. __
- This looked like a great place to have a picnic on a hot afternoon. __
- from falling down __
- which, according to my friend, is haunted. It would be a scary place to visit __ with friends late at night. __
- completely covered with snow __
- he was going very slow __

A Visit to the Countryside

1. The other day, I was invited to visit my friend who lives in the countryside. Before going, I was not excited about leaving the excitement of the city, where I live, because I thought that the countryside would be boring. After I arrived, we ate lunch. Her table was placed in front of a big window, so during the lunch, we were able to look outside. My friend's house is located on top of a hill, so we could see a great view, while eating. The scene looked like this.

2. On the left side, there was a small mountain where people go skiing in the winter. _My friend said that it was the second highest mountain in the state._ At the top of the mountain, there was a ski lodge. Often during the winter, it is almost _____ _____. Also, it is a very popular _____ _____ to visit. Just below the lodge, I could see someone skiing. I don't think that he was very good because _____. Also, he was all white with snow _____. At the bottom of the mountain was a forest of pine and oak trees. _____ _____. In front of the trees and on the left, I could see an old house _____ _____ _____. In the middle of the scene, there was a man with a horse. _____ _____. The man was dressed like a cowboy, and the horse

seemed to understand what he was saying. Also, there was a road going from the middle in the front to the upper-right side of the scene. The road was going to a house, which was located on top of the hill on the right side. _____ _____. It was a sunny day with white clouds and a blue sky. It looked beautiful!

3. In conclusion, my day in the countryside turned out to be surprisingly enjoyable. I knew the countryside would be beautiful with mountains, forests and open spaces. However, I did not realize that there could be so many things to do, like skiing, horseback riding, swimming, and even seeing ghosts.

Final draft assignment

Now write a second and final draft of the essay you have written describing the scene you drew on page 5. On page 8, you wrote your first drafts of your introduction and conclusion. On page 9, you wrote a first draft of the middle paragraph describing the scene. Now, following strategies 6, 7, and 8, rewrite all three paragraphs adding details..

Grammar Groups: *For practice with Prepositions, do Grammar Unit 4 in Section 3.*
Grammar: *For individual practice with* **Prepositions,** *do Grammar Unit 5 in Section 3.*

Essay 2: *Describing a Person*
Part 1: *Focusing on the unique features*

Exercise 1:
- ❶. Write **Physical** next to the *one sentence* that describes a person's appearance.
- ❷. Write **Character** next to the *three sentences* that describe a person's personality, talents, skills, or habits.

physical   1. She had long, silky, brown hair.

character   2. She was very proud of her hair.

_____ 3. He spent most of his weekends studying alone in the library.

_____ 4. Becasue of his large muscles, his shirts always looked like they would tear open.

_____ 5. If nobody paid attention to him, he would start trouble.

_____ 6. She makes her own clothes and jewelry.

Exercise 2:

Write one of the following characteristics in the blanks next to the twelve sentences below. Use each type four times.
- **personality** (something about their emotions or character)
- **habit** (an action or activity that they do often)
- **talent/skill** (something that they are good/bad at doing)

_____ 1. He is cheerful and a lot of fun.

_____ 2. She spends her weekends going to parties.

_____ 3. He is an excellent cook.

_____ 4. He smokes continuously.

_____ 5. She can repair all kinds of electrical appliances.

_____ 6. He is often in a bad mood.

_____ 7. He can ride horses like a cowboy.

_____ 8. She got angry for no good reason.

_____ 9. He is always looking at himself in the mirror.

_____ 10. She is a nervous person.

_____ 11. He walks very fast all the time.

_____ 12. She is a poor driver.

You write three sentences of your own that match these characteristics.

personality 13. _____

habit 14. _____

talent/skill 15. _____

Exercise 3:

Fill in the blanks with the correct characteristics from the box.
Use each characteristic two times.

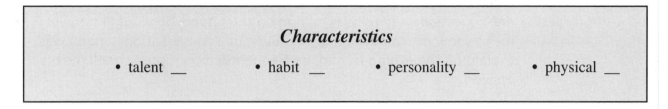

Characteristics

• talent __   • habit __   • personality __   • physical __

Characteristic

_____ 1. Even though Bob is an elementary school teacher, most people think that he is a construction worker. He is over 6 feet tall and has long, muscular arms. Also, his hands are gigantic. His stomach is flat and his shoulders are wide.

_____ 2. My brother has excellent musical ability. Often, after we hear a new song for the first time, he is able to correctly predict whether it will be a big hit or a failure. What is really amazing is that he has been able to do this even with brand-new groups who have just produced their first song. He should find a job in the music business.

Characteristic

_____ 3. I finally had to move to a single-room apartment because my roommate, Tom, was becoming too difficult to live with. The problem was that he would always interrupt me. Often, while I was reading, he would ask me a question. When I was talking on the phone, he would interrupt me to show me something on TV. Even in a conversation, when I was explaining something to him, he frequently interrupted to tell me his opinion.

_____ 4. A big problem that my neighbor has is his temper. For example, last week, he threw a magazine at his TV because his favorite baseball team was losing. His son is afraid of him because he never knows when his father will suddenly explode.

_____ 5. Dan is one of the worst drivers that I know, especially when he is driving on the expressway. He always drives too close to the car in front of him. Many times, he has to slam on his brakes to avoid hitting a car that suddenly slowed down.

_____ 6. One of my grandmother's best traits is her ability to give good advice. Because she is a good listener and because she has so much experience, she always seems to know what we should do. For example, she recommended that my brother study art, that my cousin get a pilot's license, and that I work for one year before going to college. We all followed her advice and were happy that we did.

_____ 7. This year, our city chose Dr. Cane as "person-of-the-year" because he was very generous. He not only gave money to many charities but also gave his time to helping other people. On one weekend every month, he opened his office to anyone who was poor and gave free examinations.

_____ 8. One of the characteristics that makes Robert De Niro a terrific actor is his facial expression. In many scenes, the audience can understand his emotions, for example nervousness or anger, just by looking at his face. He has several different types of smiles. Of course, one smile shows that he is happy, but others show that he is confused or that he just tricked someone.

Grammar: *For practice with* **Phrases, Dependent and Independent Clauses,** *do Grammar Unit 6 in Section 3.*

Sample essay, first draft

Exercise 1: Read the first draft of the sample essay, *"My Officemate☐"*
(***Notice:*** This is a first draft, so it is short and simple, and it may have some grammar mistakes.)

My Officemate

1. My officemate, Ann, is a unique person.

2. She is very good with computers. I was not good with them, so I hoped that she could help me.

3. She is a feminist. This means that she expects to be treated equally. She told me that the reason why she quit her previous job was because her boss treated the male and female employees differently.

4. Ann has a physical problem. She often gets a backache and pain in her wrist after working a long time at her computer.

5. One negative characteristic is that she is absent-minded. She often forgets to give me phone messages. Also, she once forgot that she had put a cup of coffee on top of her car before driving away.

6. A habit that she has is drinking coffee. She drinks about ten cups a day.

7. In conclusion, Ann upsets me because she is absent-minded, but I admire her good points. She believes in equal treatment for everyone, and she is highly skilled.

Exercise 2:

First read the "Working Thesis Statement" for the first draft of the essay above titled *"My Officemate."* Then fill in the blanks in the "List of Main Ideas."

Working Thesis & List of Main Ideas

Working Thesis Statement:
> In this essay, I will describe my officemate, Ann, who has several characteristics that make her unique.

List of Main Ideas
> 1. She is good with c_____.
> 2. She is a f_____.
> 3. She often gets backaches and w_____ p_____.
> 4. She is a_____-minded.
> 5. She drinks a lot of c_____.

Strategy 1 Choose a topic for **your** essay, think of the purpose of the essay (thesis), and think of some details (main ideas).

Write a *Working Thesis Statement* and *List of Main Ideas*

Exercise 1: Choose a topic below for describing a person.

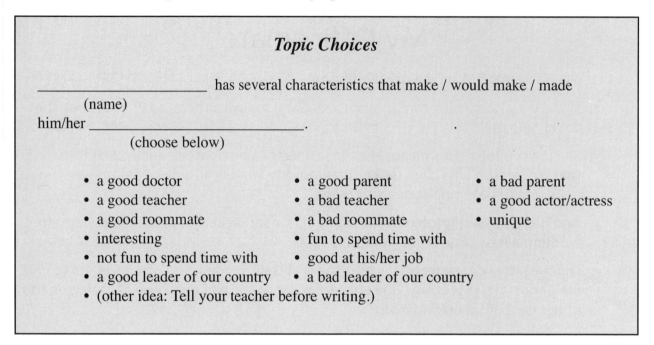

> *Topic Choices*
>
> _____ has several characteristics that make / would make / made
>   (name)
> him/her _____.
>   (choose below)
>
> • a good doctor   • a good parent   • a bad parent
> • a good teacher   • a bad teacher   • a good actor/actress
> • a good roommate   • a bad roommate   • unique
> • interesting   • fun to spend time with
> • not fun to spend time with • good at his/her job
> • a good leader of our country • a bad leader of our country
> • (other idea: Tell your teacher before writing.)

Example: My brother has several characteristics that would make him a good actor .

Example: My friend Sarah has several characteristics that make her fun to spend time with .

Exercise 2:

Write a "Working Thesis Statement" and "List of Main Ideas" for your essay.
(See sample on page 17.)

Working Thesis Statement:
In this essay, I will describe _____, who has several
characteristics that _____
_____

List of Main Ideas

1. _____
2. _____
3. _____
4. _____
5. _____
6. _____
7. (You can add more main ideas if you want.)

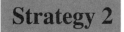

Strategy 2 Write a first draft of your essay with some details.

Exercise 1:

❶. Write a first draft for the topic that you chose on page 18.
❷. Write a short introduction.
❸. Describe some of the characteristics of the person you are describing.
❹. Write a short conclusion.

Part 3: Writing the second draft
(Think about your second draft while you do the exercises in this part.)

Strategy 3 Describe the person's talent or skill.

Exercise 1: Fill in the blanks with the correct words or phrases from the box.

• 4:50 __	• terrible at it __	• wasn't looking **𝗫**	• neither of __
• sounded like __	• angry __	• loses __	

1. My best friend in elementary school, Steve, was very good at throwing his voice. Sometimes, when our teacher _wasn't looking_ , Steve would say something like, "Hey, you!" but it _____ a student in a different part of the classroom said it. The teacher would look at that student and sometimes get _____.

2. Tom never wore a watch, but he always knew what time it was within 10 minutes. For example, we were hiking one day in the forest and _____ us knew what time it was. He told me that he felt we should start to return home because he was sure that it was about 4:45 p.m. A few minutes later, we met some other hikers and asked them what the time was. They told us that it was_____.

3. Like many people, my father loves golf. Unfortunately, he is _____. He is so bad that he sometimes completely misses the ball when he swings. I'm afraid to play with him because once he accidentally hit another golfer with his ball. Also, it is becoming very expensive for him because he _____ about ten balls every time he plays.

Exercise 2:

Choose a person and write a paragraph on a separate sheet describing their skill or talent. (Or describe a skill or talent that they <u>don't</u> have.)

Possible people you can describe		
• friend	• relative	• someone you knew a few years ago
• teacher	• classmate	• someone you see often • someone famous

Exercise 1: Fill in the blanks with the correct habit or routine from the box.

> ### *Habit or Routine*
>
> - playing with the phone cord ___
> - preparing to shoot ___
> - playing with glasses ___
> - preparing to talk on the phone ___

1. Before making a phone call, my mother always does this. First, she moves any books, cups or other things away from the phone area. Next, she puts down a piece of paper and, at the top, writes the date. After this, she takes a drink of water, clears her throat and then punches in the phone number. She doesn't like to talk on the phone, so it seems that she always needs to get prepared for it.

Routine: _____

2. It is always interesting to watch my boss when I have a serious discussion with him. If I ask him a difficult question, the first thing he does is carefully take off his glasses. While he is thinking of what to say, he blows on his glasses and then wipes them with a cloth. After that, he begins to speak, and, while talking, he puts one of the ends of the glasses in the corner of his mouth. I always wonder if he would be able to think if he didn't have his glasses with him.

Habit: _____

3. During a basketball game, players are sometimes fouled and get to shoot free throws. Whenever my favorite player is about to shoot free throws, he has this routine. First, he wipes his forehead twice. After that, he bounces the ball four times and looks at the basket. Then he looks at the scoreboard and bounces the ball three more times. Finally, he shoots.

Routine: _____

4. My sister is very active when she talks on the phone. While she is listening, she'll swing the cord around in a circle. When it's her turn to talk, she twists the cord around her hand. If there is a cup near her when she is on the phone, she'll even wind the cord around it. We were going to buy a cordless phone but decided to keep the old one so that my sister will have something to do with her hands while talking on the phone.

Habit: _____

Exercise 2: Choose a person and write a paragraph which describes their habit or routine.

> ### *Possible people you can describe*
>
> - friend
> - teacher
> - relative
> - classmate
> - someone you knew a few years ago
> - someone you see often
> - someone famous

Strategy 5 Describe a personality characteristic.

Exercise 1:

❶. Write **Helpful** next to the *three paragraphs* that have examples that help the reader understand the personality of the person.

❷. Write **Not Helpful** next to the *three paragraphs* that don't have examples, but have information that is too general and is not helpful for the reader to understand the personality of the person.

_____ 1. Tom has a temper. For example, if he doesn't like something, he gets angry.

_____ 2. Tom has a temper. For example, the other day, we were standing in line waiting to buy tickets for a movie. A man cut in line in front of us. Tom got very angry and yelled at the man. The two of them almost got into a fight.

_____ 3. One characteristic that I admire about Scott, but that also makes me uncomfortable, is his independence. Once, we were invited to a formal dinner party. All the men were expected to wear a coat and tie. Scott wanted to be different from the others, so he wore a white "Hard Rock Café" T-shirt, blue jeans and a red baseball cap.

_____ 4. One characteristic I admire about Scott, but that also makes me uncomfortable, is his independence. He likes to be different. If most people do something, he likes to do the opposite. He doesn't want to be the same as everyone else. He seems to think it is boring to act like other people.

_____ 5. Everyone who knows Jane says that she is a warm person. Because she is warm, she is very popular. She is also friendly and kind to everyone, even strangers.

_____ 6. Everyone who knows Jane says that she is a warm person. I sometimes run into her at a store while we are both shopping. As soon as she sees me, she comes up with a big smile on her face and hugs me. One time, she heard that my mother was in the hospital. She looked very sad for me and offered to help me take care of her.

Exercise 2:

❶. Choose three people to describe.

❷. Choose a personality characteristic of each person.

❸. Write a paragraph about each person with detailed examples that help the reader understand the personality of the person. To help you, here are some possible characteristics to choose from.

Personality Characteristics and Their Opposites (≠ means "doesn't equal")

- polite ≠ impolite / rude
- shy ≠ outgoing / sociable
- independent/non-conformist ≠ conformist
- angry / hot-tempered ≠ even-tempered / mild / soft
- stubborn ≠ flexible / open-minded
- talkative ≠ quiet / soft spoken
- organized ≠ disorganized   • honest ≠ dishonest
- warm / friendly ≠ cold / unfriendly
- generous ≠ tight with money / stingy
- argumentative / opinionated   • absentminded

- nervous ≠ easygoing
- cheerful ≠ sad
- feminist ≠ traditionalist
- funny ≠ serious
- extrovert ≠ introvert
- realist ≠ dreamer
- leader ≠ follower
- crabby / moody
- patient ≠ impatient
- energetic / restless ≠ lazy

Strategy 6 — Describe a physical characteristic.

Exercise 1:

❶. Write **Helpful** next to the *three paragraphs* that explain why a physical characteristic is important or significant.

❷. Write **Not Helpful** next to the *two paragraphs* that don't explain why a physical characteristic is important or significant.

_____ 1. Fred has a dark tan. In other words, his skin is brown from the sun. He is a bit lazy, so one of his favorite ways to spend the day is to lie in the sun, listening to music on his headphones. As a result, he always has a tan.

_____ 2. Fred has a dark tan. In other words, his skin is brown from the sun. His face and arms are always brown. I've never seen him with pale skin.

_____ 3. The first thing anyone notices when Karen walks into a room is how tall she is. She is almost six feet. I think that she enjoys being taller than most women, and in fact, she has some special opportunities because of it. Recently, she was offered a job as a model because of her height.

_____ 4. The first thing anyone notices when Karen walks into a room is how tall she is. She is almost six feet. I've never been in a room in which any woman was taller than she is.

_____ 5. When Ken was 16-years-old, he was in a motorcycle accident. As a result, he hurt his leg, and he now walks with a slight limp. It's very hard for him to play sports because of his weak leg, so for entertainment, he spends a lot of time playing chess.

Exercise 2:

❶. Choose *two people* to describe.
❷. Choose a physical characteristic of each person.
❸. Write a paragraph about each person with detailed examples that help the reader understand the people and why their physical characteristics are important or significant.

Strategy 7 Write a good introduction.

Writing an introduction that gives background information

Exercise 1: Fill in the blanks with the correct words or phrases from the box.

> • take care of __   • great and weak __   • by others __
> • surprised __   • excellent __   • some terrible __

Introduction 1. Most people are _____ when I tell them that I like to go to the dentist. The reason why I don't mind going is because my dentist, Dr. Wilson, not only knows how to _____ our teeth, but also knows how to help patients relax. Dr. Wilson is a woman, and she has several characteristics that make her an _____ dentist.

Introduction 2. He was loved by some Americans; he was hated _____. Almost everyone had an opinion about him. While he was president, he had some important achievements, but he also made _____ mistakes. President Clinton was a person with both _____ characteristics.

Exercise 2:

For the essay you began on pages 18 and 19, use strategy 7 and write an introduction to your essay which gives some background information.

Strategy 8 Write a good conclusion.

Writing a conclusion that summarizes why you wrote about the person

Exercise 1: Fill in the blanks with the correct phrases from the box.

- some enemies __
- skillful __
- making a lot of __
- good attitude about __
- to help him __
- either __

Conclusion 1. In conclusion, I have healthy teeth and a _____ dentists because of my wonderful dentist, Dr. Wilson. She is very _____ with her tiny fingers, and her humor makes her patients laugh. Also, she really seems to care about people and not just about _____ money.

Conclusion 2. Unlike some people, I don't hate President Clinton, but I don't love him _____. Because of his special characteristics, he was able to pressure other people _____ accomplish many things. However, because of his weaknesses, he embarrassed his friends and made _____.

Exercise 2:

Using strategy 8, write a conclusion to your essay that you started on pages 18 and 19 which summarizes why you wrote about the person you chose .

Strategy 9 Add details to your second draft.

Exercise 1: This is the second draft of the sample essay from page 17, "My Officemate."

❶. Read the essay below.

❷. Choose the type of characteristic which is described in each paragraph. Use "personality" twice.

- physical ___
- personality (1) ___
- habit ___
- personality (2) ___
- talent ___

Introduction

1   Three times in my life, I have been matched with another person. Each time, in order to make the relationship work, I needed to adjust to the other person. The first time happened when I was in elementary school, and I had to work with a partner for three weeks on a science project. The second time was when I got a roommate in a dorm at college. My most recent experience is taking place now with Ann, my officemate at the present time. Ann, the topic of this essay, is a unique person.

2   When I first heard that Ann would be my officemate, I was excited because I had heard that she was very good with computers. I was told that, in her previous job, she actually designed software and had trained her co-workers in how to use it. Because I am not good with computers, I was hoping that she could help me.

3   Nine months ago, she moved into my office and I learned something very important about her: she is a feminist. This means that she expects to be treated equally. She told me that the reason why she quit her previous job was because her boss treated the male and female employees differently. For example, even though she was better with computers than her male colleagues, her boss always chose men to be the managers. Also, he often asked her or other women to make photocopies, but he never asked the men to make them. Needless to say, this made her quite unhappy.

4   Although Ann loves computer work, it often causes her pain. For example, after she works for several hours at the computer, her back starts to hurt. Also, she gets a pain in her wrist.

5   Ann is very smart, but she is also absent-minded. Since we are officemates, we need to take phone messages for each other if one of us is out of the office. However, Ann often forgets to give me my messages or forgets where she put them. Another example of her absent-mindedness took place yesterday. Ann drove to a carry-out restaurant to get some coffee. After buying it, she returned to her car in the parking lot with the cup, put the cup on the top of the car, unlocked the car door, got in and drove off. Unfortunately, she forgot the cup of coffee on top of the car; it blew off and hit the car behind her.

6   I rarely see Ann without a cup of coffee near her. She probably drinks ten cups a day, and this has an effect on her. She often seems jittery and has trouble sitting still.

Conclusion

7   In conclusion, although Ann sometimes frustrates me because she is absent-minded and can't sit still, I appreciate her good points. She believes in equal treatment for everyone, and she is a highly skilled worker.

Exercise 2: Second draft assignment.

Either write clearly or type a second draft of your essay that you started on page 18. Try to improve your first draft by using these strategies to describe the person.

- In the introduction, give some background information.

- In the body . . .

    - Describe habits or routines that the person has.

    - Describe the person's talents or skills.

    - Describe personality characteristics.

    - Describe physical characteristics.

- In the conclusion, summarize why you wrote about the person.

Fluency Writing: *While working on your second draft, you can do a Fluency Writing from Section 2. After finishing with the Fluency Writing, you can continue working on your second draft.*

Grammar: *For practice using* **"Wish"** *and* **"Hope,"** *do Grammar Unit 7.*

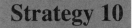

Strategy 10 Get a reaction from a peer, a fellow classmate.

Using Peer-Editing (in which the writer asks questions)

Exercise 1: Read this essay. Imagine that you have a classmate who wants your opinion about the essay, *"A Spender who is Out-of-Control."*

A Spender who is Out-of-Control

We often hear about the millions of dollars that movie stars and professional athletes earn. It seems that these celebrities never have to worry about money since they have so much △¹. Mike Tyson, a former boxing champion, made over $140 million in two years of boxing. <u>However, he was soon having troubles.</u> △² <u>Because he was unable to control his spending.</u>

One problem Tyson had was that he loved to shop. Once, △³ a store closed its doors so that Tyson and his friends could have a private "shopping party" there. They quickly spent over $250,000. He also loved cars. He bought a Ferrari for $300,000 without even taking it for a test drive. Another day, he walked into a car dealership with some friends. In the show room was a $300,000 Bentley △⁴. He bought it and ordered four more; within a few minutes, he had spent over $1.5 million. <u>Over the years, Tyson bought more than 110 cars for he and him friends.</u> △⁵

In addition to shopping, he spent a lot on his three homes. For example, it costs $100,000 a year just to pay for the gardeners. Also, after buying his third home for $3.7 million, he spent millions more remodeling it. He likes to spend money on his homes. △⁶

<u>The reason why Tyson has earned so much money.</u> △⁷ He has a lot of talents. △⁸

Tyson was a very soft-hearted person. He shares his money freely with his friends and give money to charity. Also, when his best friend is died, he is depressed for a long time. △⁹

After many years of living an expensive life-style, Mike Tyson is now struggling to save money. High-priced cars, gorgeous mansions, and other wasteful expenses have forced him to use more common sense about financial matters.

In conclusion, Tyson is an example of someone with a great talent in one area, making money by boxing, <u>and</u> △¹⁰ little talent in another, spending money wisely. When we read ____ △¹¹ rich celebrities, we can imagine many of them are probably similar to Mike Tyson.

Exercise 2: Imagine that your classmate asks you these questions about the essay. Write your advice.

1. *(Example)* Look where I wrote #1 (₍ᴬ¹₎). Should I write the word "money" here? Why or why not? *(Advice)* *No, it's not necessary because you already mentioned money in this sentence so we know what you are talking about.*

2. Look at #2. Do you think I should take out the period and make the letter "B" on "Because" a small "b"? Why or why not?

3. Look at #3. Should I tell what type of store it was?

4. Look at #4. Should I write "Bentley, the most expensive car in the world" here?

5. Look at the underlined sentence before #5. I think there are some grammar problems with this sentence. Can you help me?

6. Look at #6. Do you think this last sentence here is necessary? Why or why not?

7. Look at the underlined sentence before #7. Is this sentence grammatically correct? What should I do?

8. Look at #8. I think that this paragraph is too short. How can I improve it?

9. Look at #9. Look at my verbs in this whole paragraph. Can you tell me if they are all right? What should I do?

10. Look at #10. Should I change "and" to "but?"

11. Look at #11. Do I need to put a word before "rich celebrities?"

12. Do you think that it's necessary to give examples of other rich celebrities?

13. Mike Tyson also had a bad temper. Should I add a paragraph describing his anger? Why or why not?

Exercise 3: After you finish the second draft of the essay you started on page 18:

❶. Write some numbers on the essay in places where you would like advice from another student.
❷. On a different paper, write eight or more questions that you would like to ask.

Possible questions that you might ask to get advice

- Do you think I need more details here?
- Is there a grammar problem in this sentence?
- Do you think this sentence is necessary?
- Are my verbs in this paragraph correct?
- How can I combine these two sentences?
- Can you help me think of a way to make this clearer/more interesting?

*(**Not a good question:** Can you read my essay and tell me how to improve it?)*

Exercise 4:

➊. Exchange your new second draft papers with a classmate.

➋. Silently read your classmate's essay.

➌. Point to places on your essay where you would like advice and ask your questions. *(You do not have to make any changes to your essay if you do not want to.)*

➍. Also, answer your classmate's questions about their essay.

(Just discuss your advice. You do **not** have to write your advice.)

Exercise 5: Final draft assignment.

Write your final draft. If you want, use some of the ideas that your peer-editing partner recommended.

Grammar: *For practice with* **"Who" Clauses,** *do Grammar Unit 8.*

Teachers: see the Teacher's Manual for photocopyable:

- Description Essay Check-list
- Description Essay Evaluation Form
- In-class Essay Topics for Description Essay

Mode 2: Narration

(A narrative essay tells a story or describes a history or series of events.)

Fluency Writing: Before starting this unit, do a Fluency Writing from Section 2, pages 112-139. After finishing, begin working individually on the following exercises.

Part 1: *Focusing on the unique features*

Transitions

Expressions for narration			
• At first. __	• After, __	• While I was ... __	• Later, __
• First, __	• Shortly after that, __	• Suddenly, __	• Soon. __
• The first thing that I did was ... __	• Around 5 p.m., __	• Meanwhile, __
• Second, __	• A few minutes later, __	• At the same time, __	
• Next, __	• When I ... __	• Finally, __	• In the end, __

Exercise 1: Underline the expressions for narration.

An unexpected thing happened while my brother was watching TV last night. Around 9 p.m., he was enjoying an exciting basketball game. Suddenly, he heard loud thunder. Shortly after that, the TV went dead. While he was walking to look out the window, the lights went out. My brother was not troubled by the storm, but he was disappointed that he couldn't finish the basketball game.

I hate sitting inside my apartment, so last weekend I went to the beach even though the sky looked cloudy. While I was driving to the beach, the sun began to burn away the clouds. When I arrived, I noticed some people playing volleyball. Volleyball is one of my favorite sports, so I went over to watch them play. Soon, one of the players invited me to join them. A few minutes later, I scored my first point with a spike. The beach is a much more entertaining place than my apartment.

Exercise 2: Mark the sentences in the correct order, marking them *a*, *b*, *c*, or *d*.

1. __ My friend drove to town in order to buy a book.
   __ After he chose a book, he paid the clerk.
   __ He walked into the bookstore.
   __ Shortly after that, he left.

2. __ I followed the same routine every weekend when I was in high school.
   __ When I was finished with that, I washed the car.
   __ Finally, I picked up my friends and we went to a party.
   __ The first thing that I did, I did my homework for the weekend.

Connecting Ideas

Exercise 3:

❶. Complete the topic sentences below.
❷. Write a paragraph for each topic sentence with details like those in Exercise 1. Use a variety of expressions for narration.
❸. Underline the expressions for narration that you use.
❹. Write a one-sentence conclusion.

One of Tom's happiest memories was the day he got his _____.

During her trip to _____, Sue had some _____ experiences.

Grammar Groups: *For practice with* **Common Narrative Verb Tenses**, *do Grammar Unit 9.*

Grammar: *For individual practice with* **Common Narrative Verb Tenses**, *do Grammar Unit 10.*

Part 2: *Preparing to write the first draft*

Sample first draft

Exercise 1:

Read the first draft of the sample essay, "*Respect for Nature.*"
(**Notice***: This is a first draft, so it is short and simple, and **it may have some grammar mistakes**.)*

Respect for Nature

My friend, Abdul, from Malaysia, told me about an experience that he once had when he was in high school.

One day, Abdul and two high school friends decided to visit a waterfall. In order to get to the waterfall, it would be necessary to hike for two hours through a jungle. First, they drove to a village. After they arrived at the village. They asked one of the old village leaders where they could find the trail to the waterfall. The old man pointed to the trail but warned them to show respect to the jungle gods while they were in the jungle. They started their hike. Hiking is good exercise, so Abdul liked to hike often. While they were walking, they laughed loudly. Two hours later, they arrived at the falls. They had a good time. Soon, it was time to return home. They were walking back. It suddenly became foggy. A few minutes later, Abdul got lost. After walking for three hours, he found that he was going in circles. Night came and Abdul realized that he would have to spend the night in the jungle. He was very afraid. Meanwhile, his friends arrived at the village and told the village leaders that they had lost Abdul. An old man told them that the jungle gods were punishing the boys because they had been too noisy and had not shown respect. He said that they would have to wait until morning to look for Abdul. The next day, after sunrise, they found Abdul. He was happy to be alive.

Nature can be wonderful but it can also be dangerous.

Working Thesis Statement and a List of Main Events

Working Thesis Statement:
In this essay, I will tell about Abdul's story and what I learned from it.

Exercise 2:

In the List of Main Events below, write the events given in this box. Put them in the correct order. Following the example, check off the events as you list them.

Main Events in the essay, *"Respect for Nature,"*

- Got lost __
- Decided to visit waterfalls **X**
- Received old man's warning __

- Hiked to waterfalls __
- Found in the morning __
- Drove to village __
- Had fun __

List of Main Events

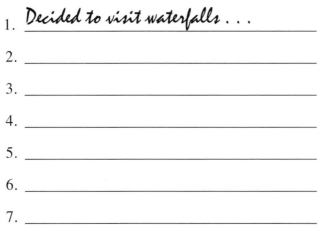

1. *Decided to visit waterfalls . . .* _____

2. _____

3. _____

4. _____

5. _____

6. _____

7. _____

Exercise 3:

In a good narration essay, the experiences should have happened within a short time (perhaps a few hours or one or two days).

❶. Read the lists of main events.

❷. Write **Good** next to the *two experiences* that happened within a short time.

❸. Write **Not Good** next to the *two experiences* that happened over a long time.

_____ **1. Kevin had an exciting experience in Hollywood.**

He saw a movie star in a restaurant.
He asked for her autograph.
While talking, they found out that they had graduated from the same high school.
She invited him to visit her at a movie studio.

_____ **2. Kevin had an exciting experience in Hollywood.**

The first day, he visited a movie studio.
The second day, he went to a famous night club.
During the next two days, he attended a film festival.
On the last day, he drove around looking at movie stars' homes.

_____ **3. During her trip to Europe, my cousin had some cultural experiences.**

In France, she learned how to make cheese.
During her week in Italy, she studied art.
She took a two-day course about German literature in Berlin.
She learned about architecture in England.

_____ **4. During her stay with a family in Spain, my cousin had a cultural experience.**

At 1 p.m., they had a large lunch that lasted over an hour.
After a little sightseeing, they stopped at a café for some refreshments.
She was surprised that they didn't eat dinner until 9 p.m.
She didn't go to bed until 1 a.m.

Grammar: *For practice with* **Reported Speech**, *do Grammar Unit 11.*

First draft assignment

❶. Now you are going to write the first draft of your narrative essay. Choose a topic *(see the suggested Possible Topics in the box below)*. Then using Strategy 1, you will write a thesis statement and list some main events in Exercise 1, below.

❷. Then in Exercise 2, you will write a first draft of your narration essay about an experience that happened within a short time (i.e. a few hours or one or two days) and explain what you learned from this experience.

Possible Topics

- Write about an experience that *you or a friend or a relative* had that was . . . *(choose one)*
    - sad
    - exciting
    - dangerous
    - strange
    - stressful
    - upsetting
    - educational
    - confusing
    - frightening

- Write about an experience that . . .
    - caused trouble
    - helped you gain self-confidence
    - influenced your future
    - taught you something important
    - helped you mature

- Write about something that you had to do even though you didn't want to.

- Write about a lie that you told someone, or that someone told you.

Strategy 1   Decide the purpose of your essay and think of some main events.

Writing a Working Thesis Statement and a List of Main Events

Types of Working Thesis Statement

- In this essay, I will write about . . .
- This paper will be about . . .
- The purpose of this paper is to tell about . . .

Exercise 1: Write a **Working Thesis** and **A List of Main Events** for the topic that you chose above. *(See sample on page 32.)*

Topic: _____

Working Thesis Statement: _____
List of Main Events:

    1. _____

    2. _____ etc.

Exercise 2: Write a first draft with the main events and some details. *(See sample on page 31-32.)*

Grammar Groups: *For practice with* **Transitional Expressions and Conjunctions,** *do Grammar Unit 9.*

Grammar: *For individual practice with* **Transitional Expressions and Conjunctions,** *do Grammar Unit 10.*

Part 3: *Writing the second draft*

(Think about your second draft while you do the exercises in this part.)

Strategy 2 Write a good thesis statement.

Writing a Good Thesis Statement to a Narration Essay

A clear thesis statement helps the reader understand what your whole essay will be about. The thesis statement is usually the last sentence of your introduction.

Notice: Your thesis statement for this narrative should tell the reader that you will write about two things in your essay:

1. tell a story
2. explain what you learned from this story or why this story was important.

Exercise 1:

❶. Write **Good** next to the good thesis statements that tell the reader that the essay will (1) tell a story and (2) explain what you learned from this or why it was important.

❷. Write **Not Good** next to the thesis statements that do not tell the reader that the essay will (1) tell a story and (2) explain what you learned from this or why it was important.

Good 1. In this essay, I will tell about a confusing experience that I had during my first week with my homestay family, and I will explain what I learned from this experience.

Not Good 2. In this essay, I will describe my homestay family.

_____ 3. The purpose of this paper is to tell about a car accident I had.

_____ 4. The purpose of his paper is to tell about a car accident that I had and explain how this experience changed my attitude about driving.

_____ 5. In this essay, I will tell about an experience that I had during a trip to Africa and explain how this experience caused me to decide to become a doctor.

_____ 6. The purpose of this essay is to describe an exciting experience that I had one day in Africa.

_____ 7. This paper will tell about my parents.

_____ 8. This paper will tell how my parents saved my life during a weekend camping trip, and it will explain how this incident taught me what a good parent is.

_____ 9. In this essay, I will tell about my vacation in Europe.

_____ 10. In this essay, I will tell the story of a surprising experience that I had in Europe and explain how this opened up a new world to me.

Strategy 3 Write a good introduction.

> ### *Writing a Good Introduction to a Narration Essay*
>
> - A good introduction for a narrative essay states some common knowledge about the topic, but it does not start the story.

Exercise 1:

❶. Write **Good** next to the *two introductions* that state some common knowledge but do not start the story.

❷. Write **Not Good** next to the *two introductions* that start the story.

_____ 1. Most people get excited before they take a trip. However, many people who travel for the first time in a plane feel not only excited but also nervous. In this paper, I will describe my first plane trip, which was both scary and exciting, and I will explain how this experience helped me become a braver person.

_____ 2. The plane took off and everything seemed normal. Thirty minutes later, the stewardess gave us something to drink. Suddenly, the plane dropped. The stewardess fell in the aisle, my drink splashed on my shirt, and several passengers started to scream. In this paper, I will describe my first plane trip which was both scary and exciting, and I will explain how this experience helped me become a braver person.

_____ 3. When I was 13 years old, I was a good piano player, so my mother wanted me to play a concert. At first, I refused, but she convinced me to do it. On the morning of the concert, I was very tired because I hadn't slept well the night before. I went to the concert hall early to practice the songs, but I made many mistakes. In this essay, I will describe my poor performance at my first concert and explain the influence this experience had on my attitude toward music.

_____ 4. My mother always told me that in order to succeed in life, we must try to have new experiences. Even though new experiences are sometimes painful, we need them to learn more about ourselves. This paper will describe my poor performance at my first concert and explain the influence this experience had on my attitude toward music.

Exercise 2:

❶. Write a good introduction for the first draft that you wrote on page 34.

❷. Write a clear thesis statement in the last sentence of the introduction.

Writing a Good Conclusion to a Narration Essay

- A good conclusion to this narration essay explains what the writer learned from the story or why the story was important, but it does not tell the last part of the story.

Exercise 1:

❶. Write **Good** next to the *two conclusions* that tell what the writer learned or why the story was important.

❷. Write **Not Good** next to the *two conclusions* that tell the end of the story.

_____ 1. In conclusion, when the snowstorm stopped, we pushed our car out of the snow bank. After that, we were finally able to drive back home.

_____ 2. In conclusion, I learned that snowstorms can surprise us. Even the most skillful driver will lose in a battle with Mother Nature. As a result, it's important for us to realize that sometimes good driving skills are not enough; there are times when we also need to be prepared to change our plans.

_____ 3. In conclusion, most people would agree that having a good friend is very important. However, we need to be ready to help our friend if we want the friendship to remain close. This means that we should ask ourselves if our friend needs our help and not just wait until our friend asks us for help.

_____ 4. In conclusion, the doctor said that Ann would recover. The next day, I visited the hospital. She looked terrible, but she still had a good attitude.

Exercise 2:

❶. Write **Good** next to the *two conclusions* that *explain* what the writer learned or why the story was important.

❷. Write **Not Good** next to the *two conclusions* that *do not explain* what the writer learned or why the story was important.

_____ 1. In conclusion, I learned that a meaningful experience is also often a painful one. Now, when I am having a difficult day, I remind myself that I can learn something from my troubles.

_____ 2. In conclusion, it was a difficult experience for me, but I will always remember it.

_____ 3. Most people occasionally have exciting experiences in their lives. I enjoy excitement, too.

_____ 3. The day that I learned that my great-uncle was a famous artist was one of the most exciting days in my life. When I got up that morning, I had no idea that I would make this wonderful discovery. It is important to remember that every day has the possibility of being the most exciting one of our lives.

Exercise 3: Write a good conclusion for the first draft that you wrote on page 34.

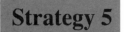 **Strategy 5** Add details to a second draft by giving more information.

Exercise 1:

❶. Read the sample first draft paragraphs below.

❷. Choosing words and phrases from the boxes (Words and Phrases for Paragraphs 1 & 2, etc.), add details to the sample second drafts. As you use them, check off the words and phrases.

Words and Phrases for Paragraphs 1 & 2

- small table __
- wildly __
- shutting __
- bedroom windows __
- noticed __
- listening to music and __

---

1. **(First draft):** After his parents left the house, his friends started to arrive for the party. Within two hours, the living room was a complete mess.

   (Second draft): After his parents left the house, his friends started to arrive for the party. *Everyone was _____ having a good time . A couple started dancing, and a few minutes later, everyone was dancing _____. Someone accidentally knocked over a lamp, another person dropped a glass which shattered, and someone else fell on a _____ and broke it.* Within two hours, the living room was a complete mess.

2. **(First draft):** As the storm approached the house, she closed the kitchen window. After that, she rushed outside to shut the windows in the car.

   (Second draft): As the storm approached the house, she closed the kitchen window. *The wind was blowing hard, so she had a lot of difficulty _____ the back door. From the window, she could see dark clouds in the sky as she ran upstairs to check the _____. A lot of dust was coming in, and as she closed the window, she _____ her car outside.* After that, she rushed outside to shut the windows in the car.

3. **(First draft):** The shoplifter went into the store's dressing room, took off his own shirt, put on a brand-new expensive one and then put on his jacket. Shortly after that, he walked out of the store.

(Second draft): The shoplifter went into the store's dressing room, took off his _____ _____ shirt, put on a brand-new expensive one and then put on his jacket. *He hung his shirt on a hanger and left it in the dressing room. He opened the door and _____ walked toward the rack with some winter coats on it. For a few minutes, he pretended to look at those until the clerk was busy with another _____.* Shortly after that, he walked out of the store.

4. **(First draft):** Because it was so early in the morning, the park was almost empty. I rode my bike on the path, enjoying the beautiful spring sunshine. Suddenly, a man with a large dog appeared in front of me. I rode away as fast as I could.

(Second draft): Because it was so early in the morning, the park was almost empty. I rode my bike on the path, enjoying the beautiful spring sunshine. Suddenly, a man with a large dog appeared in front of me. *I slowed down so that I would not hit them. The _____ started to walk up to me, and the man just kept staring at me with a strange look on this face. All of a sudden, the dog started _____ and tried to bite my leg. I _____, but the man still didn't do anything.* I rode away as fast as I could.

Exercise 2: Add details where you see this symbol: **Δ**

1. **(First draft):** As five-year-old Tommy lay in his bed, he started to have frightening thoughts. _Δ Next he jumped up and ran to his parents' bedroom.

   (Write a second draft with added details):

2. **(First draft):** After my uncle had won the $10-million lottery, the first thing that he did was celebrate. _Δ At 2 a.m. that morning, he finally went to bed.

   (Write a second draft with added details):

3. **(First draft):** Mary told John that she didn't want to see him anymore. _Δ Now, they won't speak to each other.

   (Write a second draft with added details):

Exercise 3:

   ❶. Add a _Δ where you could add details to the paragraph.
   ❷. Add details.

1. **(First draft):** My family members all arrived for the holiday party. After dinner, we did some things that we always do on this holiday. At midnight, everyone went home.

   (Write a second draft with added details):

2. **(First draft):** I had prepared for my speech very well. When it was my turn, the teacher called my name. I walked to the front of the room, but, at first, I couldn't say anything because my mouth was too dry. Finally, I finished my speech and sat down at my desk.

   (Write a second draft with added details):

3. **(First draft):** As we drove, we listened to music on the car radio. We were all enjoying ourselves. Suddenly, one of the front tires exploded with a loud bang. After the crash, the car was terribly damaged.

   (Write a second draft with added details):

Exercise 1: Imagine that the writer of *"Respect for Nature" (see page 31)* is your classmate and they want your advice about the essay.

❶. Read the questions below the essay.
❷. Write your advice about these questions.

Respect for Nature

My friend, Abdul, from Malaysia, told me about an ∆1 experience that he once had when he was in high school. ∆2

One day, Abdul and two high school friends decided to visit a waterfall. ∆3 In order to get to the waterfall, it would be necessary to hike for two hours through a jungle. First, they drove to a village. ∆4 *After they arrived at the village.* They asked one of the village leaders where they could find the trail to the waterfall. The old man pointed to the trail but warned them to show respect to the jungle gods while they were in the jungle. ∆5 They started their hike. ∆6 *Hiking is good exercise, so Abdul liked to hike often.* While they were walking, they laughed loudly. Two hours later, they arrived at the falls. ∆7 They had a good time. Soon, it was time to return home. ∆8 *They were walking back. It suddenly became foggy.* A few minutes later, Abdul got lost. ∆9 After walking for three hours, he found that he was going in circles. Night came and Abdul realized that he would have to spend the night in the jungle. He was very afraid. ∆10 Meanwhile, his friends arrived at the village and told the village leaders that they had lost Abdul. An old man told them that the jungle gods were punishing the boys because they had been too noisy and had not shown respect. He said that they would have to wait until morning to look for Abdul. The next day, after sunrise, they found Abdul. He was happy to be alive.

Nature can be wonderful but it can also be dangerous. ∆11

1. Look at the place on my essay where I marked ∆1. Should I tell what kind of experience it was, for example, exciting, sad, or frightening?

2. How can I improve the introduction? ∆2

3. Look where I marked ∆3. Would it be helpful if I explained why they wanted to go there?

4. Look at the sentence after ∆4. Is there a problem with this sentence?

5. At ∆5, what expression for narration should I put here?

6. Look at the sentence after ∆6. Do you think I should take this sentence out? Why or why not?

7. At ∆7, should I add some details about what they did at the waterfalls?

8. Look at the sentences after △8. I think these two sentences could be combined. How can I do that?

9. At △9, should I explain more details about how he became separated from his friends? Why or why not?

10. Look at △10. I want more details here. Can you give me some ideas about what he might be afraid of?

11. How can I improve my conclusion?△ 11

Exercise 2: Second draft assignment.

Write a second draft for the essay you wrote on page 34. Try to improve the essay by writing:

- a good introduction *(see Strategy 3 on page 36)*
- more details
- a good conclusion *(see Strategy 4 on page 37)*

Exercise 3: Use the second draft of your narration essay:

❶. Write some numbers on the essay in places that you would like some advice from another student. *(See Strategy 6 sample on page 41.)*

❷. On a different paper, write *eight or more* questions that you would like to ask. *(See sample on page 41.)*

Possible questions that you might ask to get advice

- Do you think I need more details here?
- Can you understand this sentence?
- How can I combine these two sentences?
- Is this part interesting?
- Can you help me think of some details that I could put here?
- Do you think that there is a grammar problem in this sentence?
- What expressions for narration should I use here?

*(**Not a good question:** Can you read my essay and tell me how to improve it?)*

Exercise 4:

❶. Exchange papers with a classmate.
❷. Silently read your classmate's essay.
❸. Point to places on your essay where you would like advice and ask your question. *(You do not have to make any changes to your essay if you do not want to.)*
❹. Also, answer your classmate's questions about their essay.

*(Just discuss your advice. You do **not** have to write your advice.)*

Grammar: *For practice with* **Which** *and* **What,** *do Grammar Unit 15.*

Strategy 7 — Write a revised draft and add details.

Exercise 1: Fill in the blanks in the following story with the correct phrases from the box.
(This is a revised draft of the essay on page 30.)

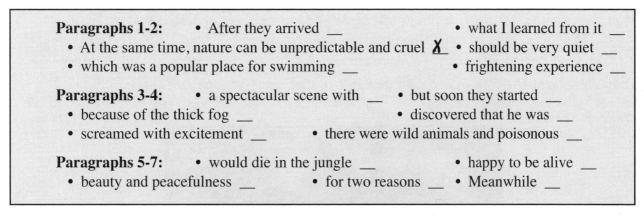

Paragraphs 1-2:
- After they arrived __
- what I learned from it __
- At the same time, nature can be unpredictable and cruel **X**
- should be very quiet __
- which was a popular place for swimming __
- frightening experience __

Paragraphs 3-4:
- a spectacular scene with __
- but soon they started __
- because of the thick fog __
- discovered that he was __
- screamed with excitement __
- there were wild animals and poisonous __

Paragraphs 5-7:
- would die in the jungle __
- happy to be alive __
- beauty and peacefulness __
- for two reasons __
- Meanwhile __

Respect for Nature

1. For people who live in a city, nature offers us a peaceful place to relax, exercise and refresh our minds. *At the same time, nature can be unpredictable and cruel.* My friend, Abdul, from Malaysia, told me about a _____ that he once had when he was in high school. In this paper, I will tell Abdul's true story and _____.

---

2. One day, Abdul and two high school friends decided to visit a waterfall _____
_____. In order to get to the
waterfall, it would be necessary to first drive to a village on the edge of the jungle and
then hike for two hours through a jungle. _____ at the
village, they asked one of the village leaders where they could find the path to the waterfall.
The old man pointed to a path but warned them to show respect to the jungle gods while
they were there. He recommended that they talk softly to each other during their hike so
that they would not disturb the jungle birds and animals. He also said that
they_____when
they were near the falls in order to experience the wonderful nature there.

3. Shortly after that, the three friends started their hike. At first, they tried to speak
softly, _____ telling jokes and singing songs.
Two hours later, they arrived at the waterfall. It was _____
the white water tumbling over a ledge, splashing into a huge pool of sparkling blue water.
The boys were so hot from their two-hour hike that they could not wait to get into the
water. When Abdul jumped in, the cold water felt so refreshing that he _____
_____. Soon, all three were splashing and jumping on each other and
laughing noisily. One of the boys climbed to the top of the falls and yelled, "Aaaiiiiaaa!" as
he dove into the water below.

4. Around 5 p.m., they decided that it was time to return. After about 30 minutes, a cloud passed in front of the sun. A few minutes later, it started to get foggy. Abdul, who was behind the other two, stopped to tie his shoe. When he looked up, he couldnít find his friends _____. He wasn't too worried though because the path was easy to follow. He started to run in order to catch up to them, but it seemed as if they had disappeared. He called out, but nobody answered. After walking for three more hours, he _____ at the waterfall again. It was totally dark by this time, and Abdul realized that he would have to spend the night in the jungle. He was afraid because _____ snakes there.

5. _____, his friends arrived at the village and told the village leader that they had lost Abdul. He told them that the jungle gods were punishing the boys because they had been too noisy and had not shown respect. He said that they would have to wait until morning to look for Abdul. During that night, the two boys couldn't sleep because they were sure that Abdul_____. They wondered what they would tell his parents.

6. The next morning, the sky was clear. The two boys rose early and started to hike on the path. This time, they spoke softly to each other as they walked. Fortunately, they were able to find Abdul. He had a lot of insect bites, but he was _____. On the way back to the village, nobody spoke.

7. This story was interesting _____. First, I learned that there are some traditional Malaysians who believe in jungle gods. Second, and perhaps more importantly, I realized that we need to have respect for nature. By showing respect, we'll be able to quietly appreciate its _____.

Exercise 2:

Answer these questions about the essay, "*Respect for Nature*."

❶. In the *introduction*, did the writer start telling the story? _____
❷. Did the writer finish telling the story *before* the last paragraph or *in* the last paragraph?

_____

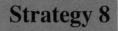 **Strategy 8** Think about your audience.

> ## Defining your audience (the people who will read your essay)
>
> If your reader (audience) is not from your country, and if you are telling a story that happened there, you might have to give extra information in your essay, so that the reader will understand.

Example Topic: Saturday night
Audience: Americans

> On Saturday night, we went downtown. There were a lot of teenagers standing outside their cars talking in the Burger King parking lot. A lot of them were out cruising between Burger King and Lincoln Park. I don't like to go to Lincoln Park in the evening because of the panhandlers.

Example Topic: Saturday night
Audience: Non-Americans (someone who doesn't know American culture well).

> On Saturday night, we went downtown. There were a lot of teenagers standing outside their cars talking in the Burger King parking lot. Burger King is a fast food restaurant. **In many towns, it is popular with young people because the food is cheap, and it has a large parking lot where everyone can socialize.** A lot of them were out cruising, **driving slowly from one place to another and then turning around and driving back, looking at other teenagers who were walking on the sidewalk between Burger King and Lincoln Park.** I don't like to go to Lincoln Park in the evening because of the pan handlers, people who ask for money.

Exercise 1:
❶. Read the paragraphs and decide who the audience is.
❷. Identify the Audience by writing **Americans** or **Non-Americans** in the blanks below.

 1. **Topic:** Childhood
    Audience: _____

> I accidentally broke a window when I was ten years old. Even though it wasn't my fault, my father didn't believe me, and he said that I was grounded for a week. I was shocked that he gave me such a terrible punishment.

 2. **Topic:** Childhood
    Audience: _____

> I accidentally broke a window when I was ten years old. Even though it wasn't my fault, my father didn't believe me, and he said that I was grounded for a week. In other words, he said that for one week, I had to come home directly from school, stay in the house and not play outside with my friends. I was shocked that he gave me such a terrible punishment.

---

3. **Topic:** College
   Audience: _____

At the beginning of his sophomore year in college, my brother was very upset. He didn't realize that when he changed his major from Phys. Ed. to Computer Science, he would need to take more required courses in order to graduate. As a result, he had to spend an extra year studying.

4. **Topic:** College
   Audience: _____

At the beginning of his sophomore (second) year in college, my brother was very upset. He didn't realize that when he changed his major (the area of study that he wanted to get his college degree in) from Phys. Ed. (Physical Education) to Computer Science, he would need to take more required courses in order to graduate. Every area of study has certain courses that students must take in order to get a degree. These are required courses. For example, Economics is a required course for someone with a Business major. As a result, he had to spend an extra year studying.

Exercise 2:

❶. Think of a topic.
❷. Write a one-paragraph story about the topic for an audience from your country.
❸. Write a one-paragraph story about the same topic for an audience not from your country.

Use this format:

Topic: _____

Audience: _____

(Tell the story ...)

Exercise 3: Final draft assignment. You wrote a first draft of your essay, starting on page 34. You added details in the second draft. Now write a final draft.

   • You may want to use some of the advice that you got from your peer editor. *(See page 42).*
   • You may want to add more details.
   • Think about the type of information your audience will need to understand your story. *(See Strategy 8 on page 46.)*

Grammar Groups: *For practice with* **Commas** *and* **Periods**, *do Grammar Unit 16.*

Grammar: *For individual practice with* **Commas** *and* **Periods**, *do Grammar Unit 17.*

Teachers: see the Teacher's Manual for photocopyable:
   • Narration Essay Check-list
   • Narration Essay Evaluation Form
   • In-class Essay Topics for Narration Essay

Mode 3: Exposition

(An expository essay defines or explains the meaning or intent of something such as a situation or idea.)

Fluency Writing: Before starting this unit, do a Fluency Writing from Section 2, pages 112-139. After finishing, begin working individually on the following exercises.

Part 1: *Focusing on the unique features*

Transitions

Transitional Expressions for Exposition		
• First. __	• Also, __	• Last, __
• First of all, __	• In addition, __	• Most important, __
• To begin with, __	• Second, __	• Most important of all, __
	• Third, __	• Finally, __

Exercise 1: Underline the transitional expressions.

Seattle is a city with some unusual characteristics. First of all, it is built on many hills. Also, the weather is not extreme. Finally, the city has a cosmopolitan atmosphere.

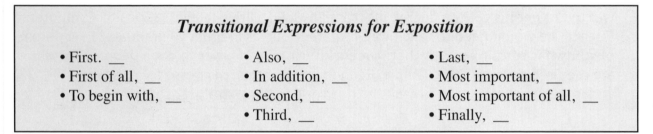

There are several reasons why travel to foreign countries is stimulating. First, in foreign countries, people can see new sights. In addition, meeting new people is a learning experience. Most important of all, people develop a new understanding of their own culture.

In choosing a dog as a pet, one should consider several factors. To begin with, one needs to think about the purpose for wanting a dog. Second, the size of one's home is an important factor. Last, some dogs require more exercise than others, so it is helpful to consider the amount of time which one has to spend with it each day.

Connecting Ideas

Exercise 2:

❶. Complete the topic sentences below.
❷. Write a paragraph for each topic sentence with information like that in Exercise 1.
   Use a variety of transitional expressions, at least three for each paragraph.
❸. Underline the transitional expressions that you use.

1. Yesterday was a *[typical / exciting / frustrating]* day for me.
   _(choose)
2. There are several reasons why I *[would like / want]*_____.
3. The person I would like to marry should have some special characteristics.
4. Before buying _____, we should consider several factors.
5. There are some aspects about _____ that make it a great place to take a vacation.
   _(name of a town or country)

Sample first draft

Exercise 1:

Read the first draft of the sample essay, "Handwriting Analysis."
(***Notice:*** *This is a first draft, so it is short and simple, and it may have some grammar mistakes.*)

Handwriting Analysis

There are several interesting aspects of handwriting analysis.

The first interesting aspect of handwriting analysis is the amount of details that it can tell us about others' personalities. According to people's handwriting, we can determine about 100 personality traits.

Second, the techniques used to analyze handwriting are quite amazing. An analyst studies the slant and size of letters. Also, they look at the loops, which can show whether someone has a big imagination. A trained analyst may take one and a half hours studying one page of writing.

Finally, there are some practical uses for handwriting analysis. Companies, especially in Europe, examine the handwriting of applicants. In addition, college students can find out if their roommates are good at keeping secrets. Also, couples who are dating can learn a lot about each other.

In conclusion, handwriting analysis is fascinating for several reasons.

Exercise 2: Fill in the blanks in the "List of Main Ideas."

Working Thesis & List of Main Ideas

Working Thesis Statement:
  In this essay, I will describe several interesting aspects of *handwriting analysis* .

List of Main Ideas:
  1. We can learn a lot about others' **p**_____
    a. About 100 **t**_____.
  2. **T**_____ are amazing.
    a. Analyze **s**_____ and **s**_____ of letters.
    b. **L**_____ show imagination.
    c. Takes _____ hours to study _____ page.
  3. There are **p**_____ uses.
    a. Companies, especially in **E**_____ analyze **a**_____.
    b. **C**_____ students can learn about **r**_____.
    c. **C**_____ can learn about each other.

Grammar: *For practice with* **"If"** *Sentences, do Grammar Unit 18.*

Strategy 1 Think about ideas for several topics.

Exercise 1:
    ❶. Look at the topics below.
    ❷. Choose seven of these topics.
    ❸. Write four main points for those seven topics.
      (For your final essay, you can choose one of these topics.)

Example

Topic: Recently, I've developed an interest in handwriting analysis. There are some aspects about it that I find fascinating.

Main Points
1. We can learn about personalities.
2. Techniques are amazing.
3. There are some practical uses.
4. There are correspondence courses that teach it.

---

1. **Topic:** Recently, I've developed an interest in _____. There are some aspects about it that I find *[fascinating / challenging / frightening / energizing]*.
   _(choose)

2. **Topic:** For a movie to be successful, it needs to have several special characteristics.

3. **Topic:** There are some changes that could improve *[this school/my high school/my life]*.

4. **Topic**: If I could design my own home, there are some features that I would include.

5. **Topic:** For a foreigner to truly understand [my country/young adults in my country [_____], they should know about some chracteristics of [it / them].
   _(other)

6. **Topic:** There are several reasons why I am glad that I _____.

7. **Topic:** To understand why some students are unsuccessful in school, we need to analyze some aspects of their life styles.

8. **Topic:** There are several reasons why siblings (brothers and sisters) are important to each other.

9. **Topic:** For people who would like to meet someone of the opposite sex, there are some ways to do this.

10. **Topic:** In choosing a roommate, there are some important characteristics that we should look for.

11. **Topic:** People who visit my country should understand what we consider good manners.

12. **Topic:** My major is _____. There are several reasons why this is a good one for me.

13. **Topic:** A good job has several characteristics.

14. **Topic:** *(You decide. Tell your teacher about your idea before writing.)*

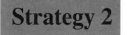 **Strategy 2** Decide the purpose of your essay and think of some main ideas.

Writing a Working Thesis and a List of Main Ideas

Exercise 1:

❶. Choose one of the topics from page 50 for your essay.
❷. Write a Working Thesis Statement and List of Main Ideas (See sample on page 49.)

Types of Working Thesis Statements (Choose one.)

- In this essay, I will discuss / explain / describe . . .
- This paper will focus on . . .
- This paper will discuss / describe . . .
- The purpose of this paper is to discuss / explain / describe . . .

Use this format:

Working Thesis Statement: _____

List of Main Ideas *(You should have more than two main ideas.)*

1. _____
2. _____
3. _____
   etc.

Exercise 2:

Write a first draft of your essay with the main ideas and some details *(See sample on page 49.)*

Grammar: *For practice with* **Adjectives incorrectly used as Verbs**, *do Grammar Unit 19.*

Part 3: Writing the second draft
(Think about your second draft while you do the exercises in this part.)

Strategy 3 Write clear topic sentences for each paragraph.

Write clear topic sentences

The topic sentence is usually the first sentence of a paragraph.
A good topic sentence introduces the main points of the paragraph.

Exercise 1: Fill in the blanks with the correct topic sentences from the box.

> • Another common technique that thieves use to rob tourists involves ketchup. __
> • First of all, laughing is very good for our health. __

1. _____. According to research, people who had heart disease were 40% less likely to laugh in funny situations than those with healthy hearts. However, we are not sure if humor helps prevent heart problems or if people with heart problems lose their sense of humor.

2. _____. To do this, two thieves work together. One of them walks up to a tourist and squirts some ketchup on the tourist's backpack and then runs away. Soon the thief's partner comes up and offers to help the tourist clean it up and secretly robs the tourist while "helping" them.

Exercise 2:

❶. Write **Good** next to the *two paragraphs* that have topic sentences.
❷. Underline those topic sentences.
❸. Write **Not Good** next to the *three paragraphs* that do not have topic sentences.

_____ 1. We can improve our physical condition by playing sports. Also, through them, we can develop friendships with people who have a common interest. Sports are good for getting us out of the house, too.

_____ 2. Going on a diet increases the chance that the dieter will start smoking. Dieting causes stress, which increases concern about weight. This often causes the person to use more weight-control methods, such as smoking. In fact, one study found that girls who diet once a week are twice as likely as non-dieters to begin smoking.

_____ 3. There is a disagreement about turning on and off computers. Some people believe that it is better to leave the computer on. The reason is that by turning it on and off frequently, we can damage it. Others say that we will save energy by turning it off if we are not planning to use it for an hour. The damage is minimal, in their opinion.

_____ 4. After waking the children up, she prepares breakfast. At 7 o'clock, she drives her son to school and then goes to work. During her lunch hour, she does some shopping for that evening's dinner. She leaves work around 5 p.m., picks up her daughter and takes her to soccer practice.

_____ 5. For example, Mt. Baker, which takes only about 90 minutes to drive to, is a great place for skiing. Similarly, Mt. Paradise is close to my hometown and is one of the most popular places for skiing in my country. Mt. Paradise is smaller, but is popular among families who ski.

Exercise 3:

❶. Write **Good** next to the *two paragraphs* that have a topic sentence and details about that specific topic.

❷. Write **Not Good** next to the *two paragraphs* that have a topic sentence but have details about more than that specific topic.

_____ 1. First, many people believe that "only children" (children who have no brothers or sisters) are antisocial. However, this is not true. Although only children are less likely to join in certain group activities such as team sports, they are just as popular as children who have siblings (brothers and sisters). Only children tend to have smaller circles of friends than children with siblings, but they have close relationships with those friends.

_____ 2. In addition, I was a college student. My major was Psychology, which meant that I had a lot of reading assignments and had to write several research papers every term. For this reason, I had little time to develop good eating habits. Another reason that I have poor health is because I rarely exercise. Part of the problem for me is that I was born with a heart problem that limits my activities.

_____ 3. One of the more interesting differences between Americans and Japanese is their use of the bathtub. It seems that Americans take baths in order to get clean, so they do not shower before getting into the tub. On the other hand, Japanese tend to take baths to relax and to warm up on cold days. They always take a shower or sponge bath outside of the bathtub so that they are clean when they enter the bath. Japanese also keep their houses clean differently from Americans. Unlike most Americans, Japanese remove their shoes when entering their homes. I have heard that this custom is becoming more popular with young people in America, too.

_____ 4. One technique that my brother uses to improve his golf is visualization. Before hitting the golf ball, he pictures in his mind how he will swing the club and hit the ball and where it will go. This technique helps him clear his mind of all thoughts except what he is trying to do, which is hit his ball well.

Grammar: *For practice with* **Adverbs** *and* **Adjectives**, *do Grammar Unit 20.*

Advanced writing technique: connecting the previous topic to the next paragraph

Exercise 4: Fill in the blanks in the paragraphs below with the correct phrases from this box. To help you choose, you will see that the topic of the previous paragraph is explained in italics before each paragraph. For example, Paragraph 2 is explained before Paragraph 3.

> - Another chimp, Sarah, learned to communicate like Washoe __
> - Not only is e-mail cheaper, but it is also easier __
> - In addition to the effects of violence on TV, there is another __

1. **Topic:** Effects of TV on children
   (Paragraph 2 discusses how the violence on TV affects children.)

   Paragraph 3:

   _____ reason why children shouldn't watch it. Children who watch a lot of TV may spend less time having conversations with others. As a result, they seem to develop fewer social skills. This could make it harder for them to make friends as they grow older.

2. **Topic:** Teaching communication skills
   (Paragraph 5 tells about a chimpanzee, or chimp, named Washoe, who learned to use sign language with her hands to communicate.)

   Paragraph 6:

   _____, but instead of using her fingers, she used a magnetic board. When she wanted to "say" something, she arranged small objects on the board. Each object represented a different word.

3. **Topic:** Comparing e-mail to regular mail
   (Paragraph 3 explains how cheap e-mail is.)

   Paragraph 4:

   _____ to use than regular mail. Let's say that I want to send an invitation to a party to ten of my friends. With regular mail, I have to write ten letters which all have the same information and address ten separate envelopes. However, with e-mail, I write one letter with this information and merely punch in ten different short addresses and then press "send."

Exercise 5:

❶. Choose three of the paragraphs below.

❷. Write a topic sentence for each of those three paragraphs.

1. _____

The most serious problem is that they probably will not have any close friends when they first move to the new town. Many children are able to make friends easily, but not close friends. They can also have difficulties finding familiar entertainment. For example, if they love skiing, but they move to a place that has no mountains, they may feel that something is missing from their life.

2. _____

For example, today most women not only decide whom they want to marry but also whether or not they want to get married. Several years ago, the parents decided when a daughter would get married and to whom. Even daughters who wanted to make their own choices were sometimes powerless.

3. _____

This is because the caffeine in coffee tends to keep people awake at night. For most people, it takes several hours for the effects of coffee to leave their bodies. A person drinking coffee shortly before bed could lay awake waiting for the effects to wear off.

4. _____

The owner of a large dog will get a lot of exercise several times a day taking the dog for a walk. Also, a large dog can be a better protector for its owner. Robbers tend to avoid houses with large dogs. On the other hand, large dogs can be expensive to feed.

Exercise 6:

❶. Think of two topics.

❷. For both topics, write a paragraph with a topic sentence and some details.

❸. Underline the topic sentences.

Strategy 4   Add details from your own experiences.

Exercise 1: Fill in the blanks with the correct words from the box.

Topics 1-2:

- try to embarrass __
- ran to the __
- Three years __
- techniques from these __
- a web site called __
- been watching __

Topics 3-4:

- a lot in common __
- After starting college __
- One day after work __
- I went to __
- I was carrying __
- began again __

Topic 1: The importance of TV

    Watching TV can have some positive points. In fact, TV once saved my life. _____ ago, I was watching a basketball game on TV. Suddenly, a message came on the TV screen warning us that a tornado was approaching our town. I _____ basement and was saved, even though the tornado destroyed the room where I had _____ TV.

Topic 2: Using the Internet

    In addition to getting information for traveling, we can use the Internet to get help with personal problems. For example, I was having a problem with my girlfriend's father. Anytime we were around him, he would _____ me by making comments about my hair cut and clothes or asking me personal questions about how I spend my free time. I didn't know how to respond to him, but I couldn't talk to my parents about this because I might give them a bad impression of my girl friend. Fortunately, I found _____ "Hey, Terra!" At this site, I could get some good advice from a counselor. I also found another site where I could tell my problems to other people my age. Although my girlfriend's father still tries to embarrass me, I've learned some self-esteem _____ Internet sites.

Topic 3: Making new friends

    A third technique for starting a friendship is to offer to help someone. I always drive to my part-time job. _____, as I was walking to the parking lot, I noticed one of my co-workers standing at the bus top. I had met him once and knew his name, but I had not talked to him much. _____ the bus stop and asked him if he would like a ride home. He accepted my offer, and we had a great conversation during the ride and found that we had _____. Soon, we became good friends.

Topic 4: Back pain

    Many people suffer from back pain and spend a lot of time and money at a doctor's office trying to get relief. I learned that there might be solutions to back pain that do not require a doctor; we just need awareness. _____ last September, I hurt my back. During winter break, the pain went away, but it returned when classes _____. I eventually realized that the cause was the heavy, book-filled backpack that _____ to class every day.

Exercise 2:

❶. Choose two topics from the list below, or from page 50.
❷. Write a paragraph for both topics. Include your experience as a detail.

Topics

1. A marriage (arranged by parents / in which young people choose their own partners) is best.

2. _____ is an invention that has had an important effect on people's lives.

3. College tuition should be free for college students.

4. There are some (advantages / disadvantages) to having children.

5. It is best to learn how to drive a car from (our family members / a driving school /_____).

6. If a factory is causing a lot of air pollution, it (should / should not) be forced to close, even if it means that some people will lose their job.

7. There are some important steps that we can take to lower the crime rate among teenagers.

8. Getting exercise everyday is important for good health.

9. Wars are the cause of many problems.

10. There are some techniques that students can use to improve their grades.

11. Old people should live (with their children / in a nursing home).

12. There are some unusual superstitions.

13. Telling a lie can have some (positive / negative) results.

14. Money does not mean happiness.

15. People who don't get enough sleep tend to make mistakes.

16. There are several ways that a (city / school /_____) can be improved.

Strategy 5 Add details by giving some information about your country.

Exercise 1:

❶. Write **Good** next to the *three paragraphs* that explain the details about information from the country.

❷. Write **Not Good** next to the *three paragraphs* that do not explain the details about information from the country.

_____ 1. Families can benefit from not watching TV. Instead of watching TV, families should spend time together talking or playing games, or even going for a walk. Also, if the TV isn't on, a family is more apt to enjoy quiet time reading. In my country, people don't watch much TV.

_____ 2. Families can benefit from not watching TV. In my country, TV programs are broadcast only from 5 p.m. to 11 p.m. The rest of the day, there are no programs, so people spend their free time talking to, and taking walks with, their family members.

_____ 3. Another good source of energy is the wind. Twenty-five years ago in my country, Denmark, we decided that we didn't want to have nuclear power. Instead, we began to rely on windmills. Now, we are getting 7% of our electricity from wind mills. By 2030, we expect this to rise to 50%.

_____ 4. Another good source of energy is the wind. Wind, unlike oil, is a good source because we never have to worry about running out of it. Also, every year wind mills are improving in design, meaning that they can produce energy more efficiently. In my country, Denmark, we use a lot of windmills for energy.

_____ 5. Competition among high school students can have not only positive effects, but also some negative ones. I've noticed a common way that American high school students try to show their superiority. It is by the clothes that they wear. Some of them spend a lot of money in order to look more fashionable than their classmates. In my country, high school students have to wear uniforms, so we don't have this problem.

_____ 6. Competition among high school students can have not only positive effects, but also some negative ones. I've noticed a common way that American high school students try to show their superiority. It is by the clothes that they wear. This is not a problem in my country because all high school students have to wear uni-forms. Because everyone dresses the same, nobody knows whose family is rich or poor. Also, students don't feel the need to buy the most recent fashion because nobody is wearing them. Although some students complain about their uniforms, most students realize the advantages.

Exercise 2:

❶. Choose two topics. *(You can use the topics mentioned on page 57.)*

❷. Write a paragraph *for both topics*. As detail, include information about your country.

Strategy 6   Add details by giving information from a source (newspaper, TV report, etc.).

Exercise 1:

❶. Write **Source** next to the *three paragraphs* that have information from a source.

❷. Write **No Source** next to the *three paragraphs* that do not have information from a source.

_____ 1. Watching TV can have some negative effects on children. I recently read an article about two similar towns in Canada. One had TV, and the other had no TV at all. Researchers found that the children in the town without TV were more creative than the children in the town with TV.

_____ 2. A third way that computers can help us is by saving time. An article in the National Post told about software that tells people when the best time is for them to get up for work. The software is programmed to collect current information about traffic conditions of any chosen roads. The information includes details on roadwork, weather and the number of cars. The computer works out how long it will take for the person to drive to work and then calls the person while they are sleeping. If the conditions are bad, the computer will wake the person up early, but if the conditions are good, it will let them sleep longer.

_____ 3. Another way to keep a healthy heart is to eat more soy products. For many years, Asians have been eating various forms of soy, and in general, people in Asian countries have a low rate of heart disease. Soy also contains fiber, which can help with digestion.

_____ 4. Drunk drivers are the cause of many deaths. Most people believe that children who are killed by drunk drivers were in a car that was hit by the drunk driver. However, according to a recent news report about child deaths involving drunk drivers, 64% of the children who were killed were passengers in the car of the drunk driver. In other words, drunk drivers are killing many of their own young family members.

_____ 5. In order to get the cheapest airfare, travelers should ask some questions when making an airline reservation. Airline workers who take reservations over the phone will look at only the specific time and date that the traveler asks for. If the traveler asks for the "lowest fare," then the reservation- taker will look at other times for better prices.

Exercise 2:

❶. Choose two topics.
(You can use the topics listed on page 57. For this exercise, *you do not have to use real sources*. In other words, you can use imaginary sources.)

❷. Write a paragraph *for both topics*. Include information from a source as a detail.

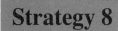

Strategy 7 Add details by giving specific, hypothetical examples, details which are imaginary (made-up).

> **Hypothetical.** A hypothetical example shows the possible or probable consequences of the topic sentence. The example is often preceded by such words and phrases as:
> "If, for example,..." "Suppose, ..." "Imagine, ..."

Strategy 8 Add details by giving general information.

Exercise 1:
❶. Write **Specific** next to the three paragraphs that include specific, hypothetical examples.
❷. Write **General** next to the three paragraphs that have information that is common knowledge (i.e. information that is generally known to most people).

_____ 1. Many people do not realize how much time is lost in front of a TV. Imagine that a person watches TV every day for three hours. In one year, he will have spent the equivalent of sitting all day for 45.6 days in front of the TV. If he did this from the age of 5 until he was 75, he will have watched TV the equivalent of 24 hours a day for 8.8 years of his life.

_____ 2. Most people would agree that watching TV can make their minds lazy. TV shows don't want viewers to become bored, so they keep a fast pace. As a result, many people come to expect their daily life away from TV to be fast paced too, or else they become bored right away.

_____ 3. Although many women work outside the home, it seems that they still do more housework than their husbands. One of the reasons for this is probably because many males and females are taught by their parents that housework is the woman's job. In traditional society, men who do housework are often considered not to be masculine.

_____ 4. Some people try to get rich by cheating an insurance company. However, insurance companies are always looking for cheaters. Imagine that a man has an insurance policy that will pay him $50,000 if he has an accident and loses a finger. If the man secretly cuts off his finger just to get the money, the insurance company will investigate his life-style before paying him. If they find that he owed a lot of money because of gambling or other reasons, they might think that he cut off his finger just to get the money.

_____ 5. Teenage girls who are on a diet are more likely to smoke. According to research, if a girl diets once a week, she is twice as likely as non-dieters to begin smoking. Imagine a girl who is worried about her weight. She goes on a diet, which causes her stress. This increases her worries about her weight. As a result, she tries more weight-control methods such as smoking.

_____ 6. Not surprisingly, the most popular refreshments at a movie theater are popcorn and soda. Some theaters are now offering some unique things such as cookies, brownies, coffee and bottled water. At one theater in Seattle, customers can buy espresso, mocha coffee and even hot tea. Still, most film-goers prefer popcorn and soft drinks.

_____ 7. More and more women are now independent enough to travel abroad alone. However, in some traditional societies, it is quite unusual for a woman to go into a restaurant by herself. Consider a woman tourist who is visiting a foreign country. She goes to a restaurant alone. If she doesn't want anyone to bother her, and if she wants good service from the waiter, it's a good idea for her to carry a business newspaper like the Financial Times. People will think that she is a businesswoman and will leave her alone.

_____ 8. In general, taking tests causes anxiety for children. To ease their stress, there are some things that parents can do. First, parents should get some practice tests and help their child with these. Next, they should explain the purpose and how the tests are scored. It is also important that the child get plenty of sleep and a good breakfast every day, not just on test days.

Exercise 2:

❶. Choose one topic and write a paragraph with general information as details.

❷. Choose two topics and write a paragraph for each with specific, hypothetical information. *(You can use the topics listed on page 57.)*

Exercise 3:

❶. Look at the sections in *bold italic print* in the essay below, *"Handwriting Analysis."*

❷. Label them by filling in the blanks with one of the Strategies for Adding Details.

Strategies for Adding Details

- From *your own experience* __
- From *other people's* experience __
- Information about *your country* __
- Information from *a source* __
- *Specific, hypothetical examples* __
- *General information* **X**

(*Notice:* This is the 2nd draft of the essay on page 49.)

Handwriting Analysis

Introduction   [1]Understanding the personality of other people can be helpful in many situations. Employers are always interested in the personalities of job applicants. It can even help family members get along with each other better. Here is a means of understanding personality that is now becoming popular in the U.S.; it has already been widely used in European countries (especially in Germany). It is Handwriting Analysis. In fact, there are several interesting aspects of Handwriting Analysis.

[2]The first interesting aspect of Handwriting Analysis is the number of

General info   details that it can tell us about someone's personality. *According to people's handwriting, we can determine if they are humorous, ambitious, self-confident, stubborn, generous, and sociable, as well as about 100 other personality traits. Although it's not 100 percent specific, we can get a fairly detailed picture of how a person will act in various situations. According to an article in* The Westerly Magazine, *"A good handwriting analyst should be extremely honest because that's the only way to help people discover*

---

their strengths and weaknesses. People can then make good use of their strong points and perhaps improve on their weak ones if they truly understand themselves."

[3]Second, the techniques themselves used to analyze handwriting are quite amazing. Using various rulers and other means of measurement, an analyst studies many features, such as the slant and size of letters. *I, for example, have very small handwriting. Tiny writing indicates that the writer is focused. My focus and concentration are so powerful that, while studying, I often do not hear the phone ring, even when I am sitting right next to it. This information helped me realize that I should probably not try to become a secretary.* The handwriting analyst also looks at loops. Someone who puts big loops on letters like "h" and "g" has a good imagination. Often, artists and actors have big loops. Apparently, imagination helps them in their creative work. Writing that gets smaller at the end of words shows diplomacy. *A friend of mine works at a store, where she is very popular with the customers. It's not surprising that she is good with people, because her handwriting gets smaller at the end of words, which shows that she is tactful.* Since there are so many details to consider, a trained analyst may take one and a half hours studying just one page of writing.

[4]Finally, there are some practical uses for handwriting analysis. Companies, especially in Europe, have handwriting of applicants analyzed. *In my country, Canada, applicants automatically include handwritten information when they apply. This makes it possible for companies to fit each employee into the most suitable type of job.* If an employer is looking for someone with a specific characteristic, for example, the ability to work with details, they could find this information from the applicant's handwriting. In addition, a college student could find out if their roommate is good at keeping secrets.

Also, two people who are dating could learn a lot about each other before deciding to get married. The couple could learn, for example, whether either of them tends to worry a lot, needs an active social life, or is sensitive to criticism. *Imagine that a couple, Tom and Sue, were considering marriage and that Tom is "the jealous type." This might mean that he would not want Sue to go out shopping or have lunch with her friends. As a result, if Sue married Tom, she might feel trapped and regret her decision to marry him. However, if they had had their handwriting analyzed before getting married, Sue would be aware of Tom's tendency to be jealous.*

Conclusion   [5]In conclusion, handwriting analysis is fascinating for several reasons. First, it can help us get some insights into each other's character. Second, the ways that an analyst evaluates handwriting are surprisingly detailed and complete. And last, it is useful in some specific situations, such as when choosing an employee or when trying to understand a friend or family member. *After all, as Reed Hayes says in his book* Between the Lines, *"Handwriting never lies."*

Exercise 4:

Optional: Write a second draft of the essay that you wrote on page 51 .
Use the strategies for adding details listed in the box on page 62.

Fluency Writing: *While working on your second draft, you can do a Fluency Writing. After finishing with the Fluency Writing, you can continue working on your second draft.*

Grammar: *For practice with* **Common Word Choice Problems**, *do Grammar Unit 22.*

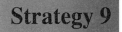

Strategy 9   Use an advanced-style thesis statement.

A **Working Thesis Statement** helps the writer start writing.
It is easy to use with a "List of Main Ideas" and in the first draft. It usually starts with:

- In this essay, I will . . .
- This essay will . . .
- The purpose of this paper is to . . .

An **Advanced-style Thesis Statement** is a better style to use
in the introduction of the final draft of an essay. For this, we do not use words
such as "In this essay . . ." or "I will . . ." or "The purpose of this . . ."

(The last sentence of an introduction is commonly the thesis statement.)

Exercise 1:

❶. Look at the topics and Working Thesis Statements below.

❷. Choose an Advanced-style Thesis Statement from the box to match each topic and write it in the blank.

Advanced-style Thesis Statements

- When passengers request a seat on an airplane, they may want to consider several factors before making their choice. __
- If we are interested in designing a house, we should follow these important steps. __
- There are several reasons why some people buy a new car every three years. __
- The health-care system in my country has some strengths and weaknesses. __

---

1. **Topic:** Buying a new car

   Working Thesis Statement *(in the first draft)*: This essay will focus on the reasons why some people buy a new car every three years.

   Advanced-Style Thesis Statement *(in the final draft)*: _____

   _____

2. **Topic:** Choosing a good seat on an airplane

   Working Thesis Statement *(in the first draft)*: In this essay, I will explain some factors that passengers should consider when they request a seat on an airplane.

   Advanced-Style Thesis Statement *(in the final draft)*: _____

   _____

---

3. **Topic:** Health care

   Working Thesis Statement *(in the **first** draft)*: The purpose of this essay is to explain the strengths and weaknesses of the health-care system in my country.

   Advanced-Style Thesis Statement *(in the **final** draft)*: _____

   _____

4. **Topic:** Designing a house

   Working Thesis Statement *(in the **first** draft)*: This paper will discuss the steps that we should take to design a house.

   Advanced-Style Thesis Statement *(in the **final** draft)*: _____

   _____

Exercise 2:

   ❶. Write **Working Thesis** next to the *three sentences* that are Working Thesis Statements.
   ❷. Write **Advanced-Style** next to the *four sentences* that are Advanced-style Thesis Statements.

_____1. In this essay, I will explain some things that we need in order to successfully travel abroad.

_____2. A good father has some important characteristics.

_____3. There are various reasons why some people are often in a bad mood.

_____4. This paper will explain the important aspects of a good book.

_____5. The purpose of this paper is to describe the harmful effects of smoking and explain how we can stop this habit.

_____6. A bedroom should have three conditions for a good night's sleep.

_____7. There are some special features of my car and some reasons why I like them.

Exercise 3: Write an Advanced-style Thesis Statement.

1. **Topic:** Police

   Working Thesis Statement *(in the first draft):* In this essay, I will explain how the police in my country are different from those is the U.S.

   Advanced-Style Thesis Statement *(in the final draft):* _____

   _____

2. **Topic:** Accident

   Working Thesis Statement *(in the first draft):* This essay will focus on the steps that we should follow if we are the first to arrive at the scene of a car accident.

   Advanced-Style Thesis Statement *(in the final draft):* _____

   _____

3. **Topic:** Cigarettes

   Working Thesis Statement *(in the first draft):* The purpose of this essay is to explain some factors that we should consider before deciding to take up smoking.

   Advanced-Style Thesis Statement *(in the final draft):* _____

   _____

Exercise 4:

❶. Choose three topics. (Some possible topic choices are listed on page 57.)
❷. Write a **Working Thesis Statement** and an **Advanced-style Thesis Statement** for each topic.

Use This Format

Topic: _____

Working Thesis Statement: _____

Advanced-style Thesis Statement: _____

Grammar: *For practice with* **Verbs followed by Infinitives** *and* **Verbs followed by Gerunds**, *do Grammar Unit 23.*

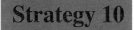 **Strategy 10** Write an interesting introduction.

Three Common Types of Introductions

- General information
- Your experience with the topic
- News (from a newspaper, TV report, friend, etc.)

Exercise 1:

❶. Read the introductions.

❷. Write the types of introductions (from the box above) which are used.

1. **Topic:** E-mail

   Introduction type: _____

   (Introduction) The first thing I do every morning, even before eating my breakfast, is to check my e-mail. My day is often affected by the e-mail messages that I receive in the morning. These messages can change not only my schedule for the day, but also my attitude.

   _____

   _____

   _____

2. **Topic:** Weather

   Introduction type: _____

   (Introduction) This summer, according to the newspaper, the eastern United States has been suffering from extremely high temperatures. Meanwhile, the Northwest has been cooler than normal. At the same time, in Las Vegas, in the Southwest, they have experienced unusual amounts of sudden rainfall.

   _____

   _____

   _____

3. **Topic:** Homes

   Introduction type: _____

   (Introduction) Two important necessities in our lives are food and home. Many of us spend a lot of time thinking about our meals; we try to prepare ones that are nutritious yet taste good. However, people seem to spend less time considering the quality of their homes.

   _____

   _____

   _____

Exercise 2:

Read the introductions in Exercise 1 again. Then choose the correct thesis statements below and write them on the last line of the introductions.

Thesis Statements

- There are several reasons why the weather has been strange recently.
- To improve our home-life, we can make some simple changes to our houses.
- E-mail can have positive and negative effects on our attitude.

First sentences commonly used by **lower-level writers**

Avoid using obvious first sentences in your introduction. These are samples of first sentences that advanced-writers usually do **not** use:

- There are many beautiful places in the world.
- Everyone has a family, and I do too.
- There are four seasons in a year.
- There are many types of people in the world.

Exercise 3:

❶. Choose three topics from the list below.
❷. For each one, choose one of the Introduction Types:

General Information, Your Experience, News

❸. Write the introduction type that you chose.
❹. Write an **introduction** and **thesis statement** only. Do *not* write the whole essay.
❺. Underline your thesis statements.

Use this format:

Topic: _____
Introduction Type: _____
Introduction & Thesis Statement: _____ . . .

Topics

• computers	• vacations	• music	• money
• bad habits	• car accidents	• teachers	• stress
• clubs	• fast food	• dating	• time
• nature	• emotions	• dreams	• (*your choice*)

Strategy 10   Write an interesting conclusion.

> ### Two Common Types of Conclusions
> - A *summary* of the main ideas
> - The reasons why this information is *important* or interesting

Exercise 1:

❶. Read the conclusions.

❷. Write the type of conclusions (from the box above) which are used.

1. **Conclusion type:** ___*Summary*___

In conclusion, to have a safe and enjoyable canoe trip, we should be prepared. First, we have to have good equipment. Second, we need to understand how to use that equipment. Third is knowing what to do in case of an emergency. And finally, we should use common sense.

2. **Conclusion type:** ___*Important*___

For people who are worried about traveling in an airplane, it's important to know that many more people have died from car accidents than airplane crashes. In fact, since 1984, fewer than 13,000 people have died in airplane accidents. Three times that many Americans lose their lives in automobile accidents in one year.

3. **Conclusion type:** _____

In conclusion, if a child behaves badly, we cannot just blame the parents. Most children try to act like their friends in order to be accepted by them. If their friends act badly, the child will probably do the same. This is why it is important for children to spend time with other children who will have a positive influence on them.

4. **Conclusion type:** _____

Although some people feel that studying stars is a waste of time and money, there are some useful purposes for it. To begin with, by studying stars, we can understand the origin of the earth. Also, it's a way to possibly learn about our future. Lastly, through this, we may find out that we are not the only living beings in the universe.

5. **Conclusion type:** _____

There are many opportunities for someone who would like to volunteer. A nature-lover can help develop hiking trails. Also, someone interested in health care can volunteer in a nursing home. Moreover, if a person likes children, many schools would like to have class assistants.

5. **Conclusion type:** _____

   As explained above, there is a good way of controlling insects. We do not have to hurt our environment in order to get rid of harmful ones. Farmers do not have to rely on chemicals to protect their plants. The safest way is to bring in helpful bugs to kill the harmful ones. If everyone who grows plants would use this method, our environment could be a much cleaner place to live.

Good Summary Conclusions

- A **weak** summary conclusion *just repeats the words* in the topic sentences.
- A **good** summary conclusion repeats the ideas but uses *different* words.

Exercise 2:

❶. Read the topic sentences.
❷. Write Weak or Good at the end of each summary conclusion.

1. **Topic:** Preparing to quit a job

   Topic sentences of the essay:

   - First, they need to have some money saved.
   - Second, it's important to learn new skills.
   - Third, they should try to keep a good relationship with their old boss.

   Write **Weak** or **Good** at the end of each summary conclusion that *does not just repeat* the topic sentences.

   a. In conclusion, if people are well prepared, quitting their job will not be so hard. First, they need to have some money saved. Second, itís important to learn new skills. Third, they should keep a good relationship with their boss. _____

   b. In conclusion, if people are well prepared, quitting their job will not be so hard. By having extra money in the bank, they will have something to live on. Also, if people continue to study and develop, they will find new job opportunities. Finally, their boss can help them if they continue to remain on good terms with him. _____

---

2. **Topic:** Things to do while sitting in a traffic jam

   Topic sentences of the essay:

   - To begin with, drivers can listen to "Books on Tape."
   - Also, they can do crossword puzzles.
   - In addition, it's a good chance to practice relaxation techniques, like meditation.

   Write **Weak** or **Good** at the end of each summary conclusion

   a. Most people hate to waste time sitting in traffic jams. Unfortunately, people who work in a city often have to. To pass their time doing something useful, drivers can learn a foreign language or enjoy a story on their tape player, or they can exercise their minds with crossword puzzles. In addition, something that will actually help their health is to practice ways to remain calm during this situation. _____

   b. Most people hate to waste time sitting in traffic jams. Unfortunately, people who work in a city often have to. One thing that they can do is listen to "Books on Tape". Also, they can do crossword puzzles. Finally, they can practice relaxation techniques like meditation. _____

3. **Topic:** Things that we should know about shyness

   Topic sentences of the essay:

   - First of all, shy people are too concerned about themselves.
   - In addition, there are symptoms of shyness: sweating, dry mouth, pounding heart.
   - Moreover, people who are shy may have problems in social and work situations.
   - Finally, it is possible to overcome shyness.

   Write **Weak** or **Good** at the end of each summary conclusion

   a. In conclusion, I was shy when I was a child. Like most shy people, I often worried about myself. Also, I suffered from typical shyness symptoms. I, too, had few friends and didn't get job promotions. Fortunately, I learned some techniques that helped me become more outgoing. _____

   b. In conclusion, shy people are too concerned about themselves. They suffer from symptoms like sweating and a pounding heart. Many of them may have problems in social and work situations. Fortunately, people can overcome their shyness. _____

Exercise 3:

❶. Choose one of the two topics below.

❷. Write a good summary conclusion for the topic.

1. **Topic:** A good restaurant

   Topic sentences of the essay:

   - To begin with, a good restaurant has an attractive appearance.
   - Also, the prices are reasonable.
   - In addition, the service is friendly.
   - Most important of all, the food is well prepared.

   Conclusion:

2. **Topic:** Saving money

   Topic sentences of the essay:

   - One way to save is to cut out discount coupons for food from a newspaper and buy clothes when they are on sale.
   - Another way is to rent videos instead of going to movie theaters.
   - As a third method, we can travel during the off-season when the prices of hotels and airlines are cheaper.

   Conclusion:

Grammar: *For practice with* **Verbs + Prepositions**, *do Grammar Unit 24.*

Exercise 4: Third draft

➀. Write another draft of your essay that began on page 50 and revised on page 64.

➁. Improve your essay by writing details using these strategies:

- Telling about your experience
- Telling about other people's experience
- Telling information from your country
- Telling information from a source
- Telling an imaginary story or situation
- Telling general information

➂. Write a good introduction using one of these types:

- General information
- Your experience with the topic
- News (from a newspaper, TV report, friend etc.)

➃. Write a good conclusion using one of these types:

- A summary of the main ideas
- The reasons why this information is important or interesting

Exercise 5: Exchanging advice on your third draft.

❶. Listen to your partner read your essay to you.

❷. After you have finished your draft:
   - Exchange papers with a classmate.
   - Silently read your classmate's essay.
   - Read your classmate's essay aloud to them.
   - Your classmate will read your essay aloud to you. You can ask them to stop reading at any time, and you can ask "peer-editing"-type questions.
   (You do not have to make any changes to your essay if you do not want to.)

❸. Also, answer your classmate's questions about their essay.

Exercise 5:

Optional: Write a final draft of the essay that you began on page 51 .

Grammar Groups: *For a review of* **Phrases and Clauses**, *do Grammar Unit 25.*

Teachers: see the Teacher's Manual for photocopyable:
- Expository Essay Check-list
- Expository Essay Evaluation Form
- In-class Essay Topics for Expository Essay

Unit 4: Comparison and Contrast Essay

Part 1: Focusing on the unique features

Expressions

Expressions for showing similarities

- Similarly, ___
- Likewise, ___
- both ... and ... ___
- not only ... but also ... ___
- also ___
- too ___

Exercise 1: Underline the expressions for showing similarities.

❶. I have never seen Tom wear anything but blue jeans and T-shirts. Likewise, Ken prefers to wear casual clothes, even to work.

❷. Both my father and uncle are bald.

❸. I have traveled to many countries. Similarly, my roommate has visited many areas of the world.

❹. During fall in many parts of the U.S., we can find maple trees changing from green to yellow and red. In my country, we can also see beautiful colors in autumn.

Impress the reader with varied style

Exercise 2: Use a varied sentence style to complete the sentences.

> *Examples* (**boring style**): I like ice cream. Similarly, Frank *likes ice cream.*
> (**better style**): I like ice cream. Similarly, Frank *enjoys having ice cream when he's hungry for something sweet.*

1. My brother is very funny.
   (use: my cousin / Likewise)

   Likewise, my cousin is good at telling jokes.

2. Air pollution is a big problem in Los Angeles.
   (use: London / also)

   _____

---

3. If you go to the French restaurant, *Mini Paris,* on a Saturday night without a reservation, you probably won't get a table.
(use: *Tokyo House* / Similarly)

_____

4. Jogging is good for people who want to develop a strong heart and lose weight.
(use: swimming / too)

_____

5. Near the end of the movie, *Gone with the Wind,* many people in the audience started to cry.
(use the movie: *Titanic* / also)

_____

Exercise 3:

❶. Choose three of the topics below.
❷. Write *two sentences for each* showing similarities.
   Use "varied sentence styles," like those in Exercise 2 above.

Topic choices:

- 2 countries
- 2 animals
- 2 courses in school
- 2 vacation places

- 2 relatives
- 2 types of food
- 2 friends
- 2 languages

- 2 movies
- 2 bad habits
- 2 clubs
- 2 colleges

Grammar: *For practice with* **-ing** *and* **-ed Adjectives,** *do Grammar Unit 26.*

Essay: *Comparison and Contrast* • **Part 1:** *Focusing on the unique features* • 77

Expressions

> ### *Expressions for Showing Differences*
>
> - however,
> - on the other hand,
> - nevertheless,
>
> - but
> - unlike*
> - in contrast,
>
> - different from
> - although
> - while
>
> *Notice: *Unlike* is a preposition, so we use the pattern: *Unlike* + noun.
>
> Unlike winter, summer is hot.

Exercise 1: Underline the expressions for showing differences.

1. My friend Ann always brings gifts whenever she visits my home. On the other hand, Ken rarely has a present for me.

2. May Day (May 1) is a popular holiday in many countries, but in the U.S., it is not celebrated by many people.

3. Soccer fans are different from a ballet audience. Unlike the soccer fans, who are usually noisy during the match, the audience at a ballet sits quietly.

4. Some people feel an IBM computer is better because a lot of software fits it. Nevertheless, other people prefer an Apple computer because it is easier to learn how to use.

5. For my uncle, the telephone is an important connection to the outside world. In contrast, my aunt uses the Internet to communicate.

Impress the reader with varied sentence style

Exercise 2: Use a varied sentence style to complete the sentences.

> *Examples* (**boring style**):   Roger lives in a large house, while *Bill lives in a small style house.*
> (**better style**):   Roger lives in a large house, while *Bill's house is small.*

1. My brother watches a lot of TV, especially sports programs.
   (use: *my sister / On the other hand*)
   On the other hand, my sister spends most of her free time reading.

2. Our history teacher made us feel nervous because he was very strict.
   (use: *our math teacher / However*)

_____

3. There are many problems with crime in Park City.
   (use: *Oakville / On the other hand*)

   _____

4. Traveling by train is different from traveling by plane. A train is slower, but the passengers have more room to relax.
   (use: *plane / In contrast*)

   _____

5. It is expensive to spend a week at a resort hotel.
   (use: *camping in a tent / However*)

   _____

6. Fast food does not have many vitamins.
   (use: *home-cooked food / Unlike*) [***Remember:*** Unlike *is a preposition:* Unlike + *noun]*

   _____

Exercise 3:
   ❶. Choose three of the topics.
   ❷. Write *two sentences for each* showing differences.
      Use "varied sentence styles," like those in Exercise 2 above.

Topic choices:

- 2 countries
- 2 animals
- 2 courses in school
- 2 vacation places

- 2 relatives
- 2 types of food
- 2 friends
- 2 languages

- 2 movies
- 2 bad habits
- 2 clubs
- 2 colleges

Grammar: *For practice with* **Comparisons,** *do Grammar Unit 27.*

Essay Patterns

Pattern: **Point-by-Point**

Example topic: My high school and my college

1. Class time
   a. High school: 8 a.m. to 2:30 p.m.
   b. College: 8 a.m. to 9 p.m.

2. School size
   a. High school: 600 students
   b. College: 7,000 students

3. After class activities
   a. High school: sports and clubs
   b. College: studying in the library

Pattern: **Block**

Example topic: My high school and my college

1. High school

   a. Class time: 8 a.m. to 2:30 p.m.
   b. School size: 600 students
   c. After class activities: sports and clubs

2. College

   a. Class time: 8 a.m. to 9 p.m.
   b. School size: 7,000 students
   c. After class activities: studying in the library

Exercise 1

❶. Read the list of ideas.

❷. Write the type of pattern: *Point-by-Point* or *Block*.

Topic 1: Two great athletes

1. Mohammed Ali
   a. Sport: boxing
   b. Prize: won a gold medal at the Olympics
   c. Era: 1960s & 1970s

2. Michael Jordan
   a. Sport: basketball
   b. Prize: won a gold medal at the Olympics
   c. Era: 1980s & 1990s

Pattern: _____

Topic 2: Two books: *Train to Nowhere* and *Blue Lakes*

1. Type of story

    a. *Train to Nowhere*: mystery

    b. *Blue Lakes:* adventure

2. Place where the story happened

    a. *Train to Nowhere:* Europe

    b. *Blue Lakes:* Canada

3. Main characters

    a. *Train to Nowhere:* detective

    b. *Blue Lakes:* husband and wife

4. Readers

    a. *Train to Nowhere:* teenagers

    b. *Blue Lakes:* middle-aged women

Pattern: _____

Exercise 2:

❶. Choose two of the topics below.

❷. For one topic, write a list of ideas using **Block** pattern.

❸. For the other topic, write a brief list of ideas using **Point-by-Point** pattern.

Topic choices:

- 2 places you have lived
- 2 holidays
- 2 teachers

- 2 types of music
- 2 movies
- 2 sports

- 2 music groups
- 2 famous people
- 2 friends

Strategy 1	Write some interview questions about your topic.

Exercise 1:

Read the *"Situation"* and *"Interview Questions"* below for Sample Essay 1.

Situation: In a few months, I will have to choose between two colleges to attend. I'm not sure which one will be best for me, so I will interview two students who attend these colleges in order to get more information.

Interview Questions for Sample Essay 1:

Comparing State University to Border College

1. How many students attend the college?

2. Do you like the size? Why (not)?

3. Are there many computer labs?

4. What does the campus look like?

5. What subjects can I study there?

6. *(Specific example question)* Can you tell me some examples of what students do when they are not in class?

7. How big are the classes?

8. *(Narrative question)* Can you tell me about an experience that you had with a professor?

9. Can you describe the dorms or apartments where the students live?

10. Can you describe the environment outside the campus? Is there a city or nature nearby?

11. *(Narrative question)* Can you tell me about an experience that you had with another student at your school?

Sample first draft essay 1

After preparing the eleven questions above, the writer used them to interview two students, Tom and Sara, and then wrote the first draft of the essay on the next page.

Exercise 2:

Read the first draft of the sample essay below, "Two Colleges." (*Notice: This is a first draft, so it is short and simple, and it may have some grammar mistakes.*)

Two Colleges (first draft)

¹ I am planning to attend college next year, but I'm not sure which college is best for me. I decided to interview two people, Tom and Sara, who attend two different colleges in order to help me make the choice.

² State University (SU), which Tom goes to, is a large college. About 14,000 students attend it. He says that he thinks the large size makes campus life exciting. He also likes the atmosphere. By this, I mean that it seems like a college that we see in movies and read about in books. Many of the buildings are over 100 years old and have ivy covering the walls. His favorite place is a large grassy area called the Quad that almost looks like a park. According to Tom, on warm sunny days, the Quad is filled with students sitting on blankets, playing Frisbee, or just talking with friends. He said that his best college memories are about the times that he spends in the Quad. In fact, this is where he met his girlfriend.

³ Although there are often more than 100 students in a class at SU, the quality of education is outstanding because of the great teachers. Some of the professors are world-famous. Tom told me about an unusual experience he once had with his Asian History professor. About half-way through the term, he had trouble understanding one of the lectures, so he made an appointment to see the professor in his office. When Tom arrived for his appointment, the professor wasn't there. Tom waited for an hour and then wrote an angry note to the professor and put it on his office door. That evening, Tom opened the newspaper, and to his surprise, there was a picture of his professor sitting next to the president of the United States. According to the newspaper, the president had just asked the professor to rush to Washington D.C. to help him with an emergency situation in Asia. After reading the article, Tom ran to the professor's office and took back his angry note.

⁴ I asked Tom about the surroundings, in other words, how students spend time off campus. He said that there is a small town nearby where students can shop, but there isn't much to do there. To get to a large city, he has to drive about two hours.

⁵ After talking to Tom about SU, I interviewed Sara about her college, Border College. Unlike SU, Border College is quite small, with only about 2,000 students. While it is similar to SU with old, traditional buildings, the campus is small. Sara felt that the small size is an advantage because it was easy to find classrooms and doesn't take a long time to walk from one end of the campus to another.

⁶ In contrast to SU, Border College (BC) has a small number of students (about 25) in each class. Sara said that, because the classes are so small, she gets many chances to speak and ask questions. This has helped her a lot. Although the professors are not world-famous, they are friendly and always willing to help students after classes.

⁷ The environment that surrounds BC is different from SU's. There is a busy town 10 minutes away on foot from campus. Besides good shopping, the town has some interesting coffee shops that have entertainment on weekends. In addition, just 15 minutes away by car, there is a lake surrounded by forests and hiking trails. This is a great place for students who want to spend time relaxing, swimming, and exercising.

⁸ After talking to Tom and Sara, I spent several days thinking about SU and BC. SU's campus with its Quad sounded more interesting than BC's. Also, it would be exciting to have world-famous professors. However, I am quite shy, so it might be difficult for me to study in large classes. In addition, I think that it would be easier for me to get physical exercise if I went to BC. For those reasons, I have decided to attend BC.

Exercise 3:

Write the type of pattern used for the essay, *"Two Colleges"*: **Point-by-Point** or **Block**.

Pattern: _____

Exercise 4:

Notice: To write the essay, "Two Colleges," the writer did not use information from all 11 of the interview questions on page 82.

❶. Look at the 11 interview questions again on page 82.
❷. The writer used information from only 7 questions.
   Circle the numbers of these seven questions.

Exercise 5: Read the *"Situation"* and *"Interview Questions"* below for Sample Essay 2.

Situation: Jim will soon take a 12-hour plane flight overseas. He needs to choose one person to be his seatmate, so he interviewed two friends. He will choose one of them to sit next to him during the long flight.

Interview Questions for Sample Essay 2:

Comparing Two People as Airplane Seatmates

1. If you are going a long distance, do you prefer to travel by car or plane? Why?

2. *(Narrative question)* Can you tell me about an interesting experience that you had at an airport?

3. Do you like the food that is served on planes? Why (not)?

4. *(Specific example question)* What topics do you like to talk about?

5. Do you usually enjoy the movies on a flight?

6. How many times a year do you travel by plane?

7. *(Narrative question)* Can you tell me about the best or worst flight that you ever took?

8. *(Specific example question)* Can you tell me the names of some places that you have traveled to?

9. Can you tell me about your favorite place to go by plane for a vacation?

10. Have you ever become angry with anyone during a plane flight? Explain.

Physical observations: In addition to asking the questions above, Jim made some physical observations about the two possible seatmates.

1. Size (height & weight)	3. Type of clothes
2. Age	4. Smile

Sample first draft essay 2

After preparing the 10 questions and the list of 4 physical observations above, the writer used them to interview two people, Ken and Ann, and then wrote the first draft of the essay below.

Exercise 6:

Read the first draft of Jim's sample essay, *"Airplane Seatmates."* (**Notice**: *This is a 1st draft, so there are some grammar and style mistakes.*)

Airplane Seatmates (1st draft)

¹ During a long plane flight, it's important to find some pleasant ways to pass the time. Because I was planning to take a 12-hour flight overseas, I decided that I wanted a seatmate (in other words, the person sitting next to me on the flight) who could make the 12 hours as enjoyable as possible. I asked two people some questions in order to help me choose which one I preferred as a seatmate.

² Ken is likes to talking. He's had many unusual experiences, and he likes to talk about his unusual experiences. For example, three years ago, he climbed the highest mountain in the world. He also hiked across the Sahara Desert. Also, a plane that he was on was hijacked. Also, he has an opinion about everything. If someone mentions sports, politics, cars, movies, or even the weather, Ken wants to say what he thinks. He once talked for an hour about which cities had the best Chinese food. Ken is talkative, Ann is quiet. This doesn't mean that she never speaks. She has visited several interesting places, like Brazil and Thailand, but she seldom talks about them. She seems more interested in listening than talking. She often will ask a short but excellent question to learn about the other person. For example, I told her that I was thinking about quitting my job because of all the problems that I was having with my boss. She listened to my complaints silently and then asked me if I had told my boss how I felt. Actually, I hadn't, but I then decided that I should try that.

³ On an airplane, I sometimes feel uncomfortable because the seats are small. I need to spread out my legs and arms if possible. Ken is a big, 30-year-old fellow. Ken is about 6 feet, 4 inches tall and weighs about 230 pounds. When he is sitting down, it looks like he needs two seats. Ann is small. Some people think that she is a teenager because she is so tiny, even though she is almost 40 years old. She told me an interesting story about her size. One day she was at a shopping mall with her 16-year-old daughter. While they were looking at some clothes, a couple of teenage boys started a conversation with them. After a few minutes, they invited Ann and her daughter to a party. Ann didn't want to embarrass the boys, so she just told them that her mother wouldn't let her stay out after 9 p.m.

⁴ Finally, for me, one of the pleasures of traveling by plane is the food. Surprisingly, both Ann and Ken like the food served on planes, too. However, I imagine that Ann would not eat all of her meal; in other words, she would probably share her dessert with me. Unlike Ann, Ken would probably ate all of his food and even ask me for some of mine.

⁵ I am not looking forward to sit on an airplane for 12 hours. Because I tend to get bored after 30 minutes. Whenever I'm not busy, I always need something to distract me. As a result, I have decided to choose Ken as my seatmate. Although we will feel crowded sitting next to each other, and I might have to give him some of my dinner, I don't think I will mind it, because he will probably entertain me with all of his stories and opinions. I think that I and Ken will have a great time together.

Exercise 7:

Write the type of pattern used for the essay, *"Airplane Seatmates"*: **Point-by-Point** or **Block**.

Pattern: _____

Exercise 8:

Notice: To write the essay, the writer did not use information from all 10 of the interview questions and 4 physical observations on page 84.

❶. Look at the 10 interview questions and 4 physical observations again on page 84.

❷. The writer used information from three questions and two physical observations. Circle the numbers of these three questions and two physical observations.

Exercise 9:

❶. Choose one of the topics below. This will be the topic for your next essay.

❷. For the topic, describe a situation and write between 10 and 20 interview questions. (For sample situations and questions, see page 82 and page 84.)

❸. In your interview questions, include some *narrative questions* and *specific example questions*. You may want to include some *physical observations*, too.

Topics

- Compare two people and make a decision about them. *(Choose one of these.)*

  - Which one would be the better roommate for you?
  - Which one would be the better employee for you if you were a boss?
  - Which one would be the better teacher for your son or daughter if you had one?
  - Which one would you want your brother or sister to marry?
  - Which one would be the better person to take a vacation with?
  - Which one would be the better teammate for you? *(Choose a sport.)*
  - Which one would be the better home-stay guest?
    (In other words, they would stay with you and your family for a year.)
  - Which one would be the better son or daughter for you?
  - Which one would be the better person to spend a year with on a deserted island?
  - Which one would be the better _____? *(You decide the topic. Tell your teacher the topic before you start writing the interview questions.)*

Other Possible Topics

- Compare two countries or cities and make a decision about them.
  Talk to two people from different countries or cities.
  These people should not be from your country or city. *(Choose one of these.)*

  - Which country or city would be a better place for living and working?
  - Which country or city would be a better place for going to school?
  - Which country or city would be a better place for a vacation?
  - Which country or city seems more interesting?

- Do not interview anyone yet.

Strategy 2 · Write examples with specific details that help the reader understand your ideas.

> **Not enough details.** Students who have part-time jobs are often too busy to study. *For example, my friend, Tim, has a part-time job, and he is too busy to study.*
>
> **Good specific details.** Students who have part-time jobs are often too busy to study. *For example, my friend, Tim, works at his part-time job from 4 p.m. to 10 p.m. He gets back home around 10:30 and tries to study for a few hours, but he is usually too tired. For this reason, he's failing some of his classes.*

Exercise 1:

❶. Write **Good Details** next to the *five paragraphs* in which the examples have specific details that help the reader understand.

❷. Write **Not Enough** next to the *three paragraphs* in which the examples do not have enough details.

_____ 1. People who visit Hawaii can enjoy the food from different cultures. For example, a lot of different kinds of food are served there.

_____ 2. People who visit Hawaii can enjoy the food from different cultures. For instance, at Café 100 on Hawaii Island, customers can order American-style hamburgers, Korean *kim chee* and Hawaiian *lau lau*, which is meat steamed in banana leaves.

_____ 3. There are a lot of ways that we can decorate our homes so that we can get an enjoyable atmosphere. For example, my neighbor decorated his home and made a nice atmosphere.

_____ 4. There are a lot of ways that we can decorate our homes so that we can create a pleasant atmosphere. For example, my neighbor improved the atmosphere by painting all the rooms in bright colors.

_____ 5. Many people like to start their day with a cup of coffee because it can help them wake up. However, drinking too much coffee can cause some problems. For example, it can cause headaches, shakiness, and stomachaches and can interfere with our sleep.

_____ 6. Because the cost of raising children is so high these days, we are finding more and more dual-career families. This means families in which both the husband and wife work. For instance, some husbands and wives both work in order to earn enough money.

_____ 7. I read an interesting article about prison life. The writer gave some advice about how the new prisoners can survive there. For example, he said that prisoners should never borrow anything from another prisoner. Also, if a prisoner bumps into another prisoner by accident, they should say, "Excuse me," to show respect. If they don't show respect, they might get killed.

_____ 8. In the past, I always had jobs where I worked alone. Recently, I got a job which would require me to work with a group of people, so I was a little nervous. On the first day, my boss gave some recommendations for how to be a good group member. He said that I should volunteer to do some extra work. For instance, if the group needed someone to make a photocopy of some papers, I could volunteer to do that job.

Exercise 2:

❶. For each of the following sentences, write a paragraph and include an example with specific details.

❷. Use one of these: *"For example"* or *"For instance."*

1. College graduates have some advantages over high school graduates. *For example, it was reported in the news that someone with a college degree can expect to earn $16,000 a year more than someone with just a high school diploma.*

2. These days, young people feel a lot of pressure.

3. Some things in my country are very expensive.

4. Students who study abroad can expect some [problems / advantages] when they return to their own countries.
   (Choose)

5. When Ann was a child, she often behaved badly.

6. Some people are very superstitious.

Exercise 3:

❶. Choose three topics.

❷. Write a paragraph for each topic, like those in Exercise 2 above.

❸. Use the expressions, *"For example"* or *"For instance."*

Topics

- Trying to lose weight
- Learning a second language
- Good teachers and bad teachers
- Secrets
- Cheating
- Sleep
- Ending a relationship with a boyfriend/girlfriend
- *(You decide a topic.)*

- Finding a job
- Learning how to drive a car
- Computers / Internet
- Illness
- Money
- Old people

Grammar Groups: *For practice with* **Passive Voice,** *do Grammar Unit 28.*

Grammar: *For individual practice with* **Passive Voice,** *do Grammar Unit 29.*

Strategy 3 Use a narrative (short story) in a paragraph to explain your ideas.

> A **good, interesting narrative** tells the events about
> something that happened one time (not every day).

❶. Write **Good Narr** next to the *three paragraphs* that tell the events of a story.

❷. Write **Not Narr** next to the *three paragraphs* that do **not** tell the events of a story.

_____ 1. A second positive effect that pets have is that the owners can meet new people through their pets. Robert Kramer was 65 when his wife died. For the first year after her death, Robert was very lonely because he had few opportunities to meet new people. One day, a neighbor who was going on vacation asked Robert to take care of her dog. He agreed to do that and one day took the dog for a walk in a park. During the walk, he met a 60-year-old widow who was also walking her dog. Soon, they became good friends and eventually got married.

_____ 2. A second positive effect that pets have is that the owners can meet new people through their pets. Some owners take their dogs to the local park in order to get exercise. While enjoying the fresh air and activity, they have a chance to socialize with other owners and pets.

_____ 3. It is common for young people to try to travel abroad without spending a lot of money. To do this, they often stay in hotels that are cheap but sometimes dangerous. Whenever I traveled, I was always worried about a thief stealing my money from my inexpensive hotel room while I was sightseeing. I finally discovered that a good way to hide my money in my room was to put it in a plastic bag and then put it in the water tank behind the toilet.

_____ 4. It is common for young people to try to travel abroad without spending a lot of money. To do this, they often stay in hotels that are cheap but sometimes dangerous. One hotel I stayed at in a big city was only $20 a night. As soon as I entered the room, I realized why it was so cheap. The room was dirty and the lock on the door was broken. I had a lot of money with me because I had just started my trip. I decided to hide it in the room, while I went sightseeing for four hours. When I arrived back at my hotel room, I noticed my door was slightly open; someone ha entered my room and looked through my backpack. Fortunately, they didn't find my money. I had taped it to the wall behind a picture above the bed.

_____ 5. Although there are some advantages to working, women who have small children sometimes suffer from some disadvantages, too. Some of these mothers have a difficult time balancing their professional lives and home lives. I read an article about a woman named Jennifer, who was a music teacher and a mother of a two year-old son and three year-old daughter. One day she was late for work. Usually on the way to work, she drops off her daughter first at her day-care center, and then drops off her son at his baby-sitter's. However, this day, without thinking, she switched the order. In other words, she absentmindedly dropped off her son first. After dropping off her daughter, she expected to see her son waiting in the back-seat of the car, as usual. When she noticed that he wasn't there, she panicked. She was sure that he had left the car and walked off into a nearby forest. She called the police and soon a helicopter was looking for her son. For three hours, the police and 100 volunteers searched the forest. Finally, she remembered that she had already dropped her son off at the baby-sitter's. After her mistake was discovered, she felt relieved but terribly embarrassed.

_____ 6. Although there are some advantages to working, women who have small children sometimes suffer from some disadvantages, too. Some of these mothers have a difficult time balancing their professional lives and home lives. Although many husbands these days say that they want their wives to work and that they will try to help with household duties, very often, they don't do enough. The wives still have to do the majority of household duties in addition to their jobs. Many of them spend over eight hours at work and six hours taking care of their children and the household every day. They have little time to relax.

Exercise 2:

❶. Choose two topics.

❷. Write a paragraph for both topics. Include a narrative (a short story which happened one time) in each.

Topics

- Trying to lose weight
- Learning a second language
- Good teachers and bad teachers
- Secrets
- Cheating
- Sleep
- Childhood memories
- Ending a relationship with a boyfriend/girlfriend
- _(You choose a topic)_

- Finding a job / apartment
- Learning how to drive a car
- Computers / Internet
- Illness
- Money
- Old people

Exercise 3:

(Optional) Look again at the list of questions that you wrote on page 86.
Revise the questions or add new questions to your list.

Strategy 4   Interview someone to get information for your essay.

Exercise 1: Use the interview questions that you wrote on page 86.

   ❶. Choose two people to interview.

   ❷. Ask them your questions and take notes.

   ❸. In your essay, you will need to have a narrative in one paragraph. You should make sure that the people whom you interview tell you a story that you can use in your essay.

   ❹. If you don't get interesting / useful / enough information from these two people, you can interview more people.

> Your teacher may require you to interview two people
> or allow you to use your imagination instead.

Exercise 2: Prepare your first draft.

   ❶. Write a working thesis statement and list of ideas. *(See page 49.)*

   ❷. Write your first draft. You should have:

- an introduction that explains the situation.
  (See the examples on pages 82 and 85.)
- some paragraphs that compare and contrast the people or places.
- at least one narrative.
  (See examples in paragraph 3, page 83 and in paragraph 3, page 85.)
- a conclusion in which you explain your choice and the reasons for your decision.
  (See the examples on pages 83 nd 85.)

Part 3: Writing the second draft
(Think about your second draft while you do the exercises in this part.)

Strategy 5 — Use the teacher's suggestions and comments to improve the details of your essay.

Common Comments by Teachers

- Explain more.
- Give some examples.
- Explain with a short narrative.
- Too general; add specific details.

Exercise 1:

Fill in the blanks in the *"Student's revision,"* which is in **bold print,** with the correct phrases from the box.

Paragraphs A & B:
- During her year ___
- For example, she **✗**
- felt bored ___
- point of view ___

Paragraphs C & D:
- the library and computer ___
- For instance, one ___
- electricity to come ___
- Once, she was ___

Paragraphs E & F:
- as a math tutor ___
- a large city ___
- an experience that he had ___
- For example, it takes ___

Paragraph A

Teacher's comments	Sample paragraph from an essay
¹ Give some examples	**A.** When I was a child, I was very dependent on my mother. ₐ¹ As a result, I didn't have many friends. Also, I didn't learn to do things myself.
	Student's revision using the teacher's suggestion
	A. When I was a child, I was very dependent on my mother. ₐ¹ _For example, she_ would always play video games with me and take me to movies. If I ever _____, she entertained me. As a result, I didn't . . .

Paragraph B

Teacher's comments	Sample paragraph from an essay
[2] *Explain what happened in Greece that made her choose that major.*	**B.** Kelly was especially interested in Greece because she had been an exchange student there. [2] After that experience, she decided to major in International Relations.
	Student's revision using the teacher's suggestion
	B. Kelly was especially interested in Greece because she had been an exchange student there. [2] _____ *in Greece, she noticed that many Greeks had a misunderstanding about Americans. They thought that Americans wanted to force their culture on the Greeks. Kelly wanted to help both the Americans and Greeks to see each other's* _____ After that experience, she . . .

Paragraph C

Teacher's comments	Sample paragraph from an essay
[3] *Too general, add specific details. Explain with a short narrative.*	**C.** Tom studied hard [3]. Likewise, Ann made a great effort [4].
	Student's revision using the teacher's suggestion
	C. Tom studied hard. [3] *He never went to bed before 1 a.m. Even on weekends, he studied about six hours a day.* Likewise, Ann made a great effort. [4]_____ *walking across campus when a friend ran up to her. Her friend was surprised to see her. She had thought that Ann had quit school the previous term because she hadn't seen her in several weeks. The reason why nobody had seen Ann was because she was spending all her time in* _____ *lab.*

Paragraph D

Teacher's comments	Sample paragraph from an essay
[5] *Explain more or explain with a narrative.*	**D.** Susan would be good to have as a companion during an emergency. She tends to stay calm in tense situations. △[5] She is also very clever.
	Student's revision using the teacher's suggestion
	D. Susan would be good to have as a companion during an emergency. She tends to stay calm in tense situations. △[5] _____ night a storm knocked out the electricity. Susan lit about 25 candles, put them all around the living room and actually enjoyed waiting for the _____ on again. She is also...

Paragraph E

Teacher's comments	Sample paragraph from an essay
[6] *Too general; add more specific details. Explain with a short narrative.*	**E.** Doug's hometown is in a good location. △[6] However, the climate isn't my favorite.
	Student's revision using the teacher's suggestion
	E. Doug's hometown is in a good location. △[6] _____ _____ only about an hour to get to the mountains, 30 minutes to the ocean beaches and 90 minutes to drive to _____. However, the climate...

Paragraph F

Teacher's comments	Sample paragraph from an essay
[7] *Explain more or explain with a narrative.*	F. It's also easy to get a job in Frank's country. [7] In fact, there is almost no unemployment.
	Student's revision using the teacher's suggestion F. It's also easy to get a job in Frank's country. [7] **Frank told me about** _____. One spring, on the day that high school classes finished for the school year, Frank was walking home with some friends. Soon, a car drove up to them, and a man asked them if they'd like a job at his grocery store. They told him that they would think about it. When Frank got home, there was a phone message from someone else who wanted to hire him _____ _____. In fact, there is almost no...

Exercise 2:

❶. Read the sample paragraphs and teacher's comments.
❷. Choose five of these and write a revision for each.

1.

Teacher's comments	Sample paragraph from an essay
Too general; add some specific details.	We didn't want to go to that restaurant because it was too expensive. In the end, we went out for pizza...

Your revision:

2.

Teacher's comments	Sample paragraph from an essay
Give some examples or write a narrative.	Steve has a lot of problems with people. However, he is good with cars.

Your revision:

3.

Teacher's comments	Sample paragraph from an essay
Explain more.	Terri enjoys nature. As a result, she seems very calm.

Your revision:

4.

Teacher's comments	Sample paragraph from an essay
Explain with a narrative.	Tom is famous for taking risks. I worry that some day he might get injured.

Your revision:

5.

Teacher's comments	Sample paragraph from an essay
Give some examples.	Sara is very talented. I'm sure that she will be famous in the future.

Your revision:

6.

Teacher's comments	Sample paragraph from an essay
Needs more specific details.	In Dick's city, there are a lot of things to do. It's not surprising that a lot of tourists go there.

Your revision:

7.

Teacher's comments	Sample paragraph from an essay
More explanation needed here.	Kevin's country has some problems with crime. As a result, I hesitate to visit there.

Your revision:

8.

Teacher's comments	Sample paragraph from an essay
Again too general. You need additional specific details.	Jane and Sally are good friends, and they enjoy the same things. They hope to stay friends for a long time.

Your revision:

9.

Teacher's comments	Sample paragraph from an essay
Insufficient details. Add more.	*(You write a paragraph on any topic.)*

Your revision:

10.

Teacher's comments	Sample paragraph from an essay
	(You write a paragraph on any topic.)

Your revision:

Strategy 6 Use a variety of sentence styles.

Exercise 1: ❶ Read the essay in Text 1(boring style), *"A Bad Elephant,"* below.
 ❷. Look at the words that start each sentence.
 ❸. If the sentence starts with the subject, put a check in the box on the left.
 ❹. If the sentence does not start with the subject, put a check in the box on the right.

Text 1 (boring style)

A Bad Elephant

1 Everyone knows that elephants are one of the most popular attractions at zoos and circuses. 2 People are fascinated by them because of their size and unique build. 3 However, not all elephants are attractive. 4 Elephants have killed 22 humans in the past 20 years in North America. 5 It is surprising that elephant-handlers are more likely to die on the job than police officers, fire fighters or coal-miners. 6 It is the most dangerous job in the U.S., according to government studies.

7 Suki is an Asian elephant who will spend the rest of her life at "an elephant-prison" for "bad" elephants near Seattle in Washington state. 8 Her handlers treat her very carefully since she is a killer and weighs over 2,000 pounds (1,000 kilograms). 9 Special movable walls act as "separators" between her and the handlers when they care for her. 10 Suki has two elephant-roommates who are also dangerous. 11 The three elephants could leave their elephant-prison if their behavior improved. 12 However, no one expects that to happen.

13 Suki was a good elephant in her younger days as a circus performer. 14 She learned tricks easily because she was very smart. 15 It was unfortunate that one of the tricks which she learned was a headstand. 16 She did a headstand on one of her handlers one day and killed him. 17 She killed a second handler in the same way some time later. 18 Suki was finally sent to "the prison" for bad elephants after she tried to do a head-stand on a third handler. 19 Her owners were relieved to find "a home" for her, but they were disappointed that she could not perform with the circus any more.

sentences starting with the subject	sentences *not* starting with the subject
1 ✔	1
2	2
3	3
4	4
5	5
6	6
7	7
8	8
9	9
10	10
11 ✔	11
12	12
13	13
14	14
15	15
16	16
17	17
18	18
19	19

Exercise 2:

❶. Read the essay Text 2 (interesting style), *"A Bad Elephant,"* below.
❷. Look at the words that start each sentence.
❸. If the sentence starts with the subject, put a check in the box on the left.
❹. If the sentence does not start with the subject, put a check in the box on the right.

Text 2 (interesting style)

A Bad Elephant	sentences starting with the subject	sentences *not* starting with the subject

A Bad Elephant

1 Needless to say, elephants are one of the most popular attractions at zoos and circuses. *2* Because of their size and unique build, people are fascinated by them. *3* However, not all elephants are attractive. *4* In North America, elephants have killed 22 humans in the past 20 years. *5* Surprisingly, elephant-handlers are more likely to die on the job than police officers, fire fighters or coal-miners. *6* According to government studies, it is the most dangerous job in the U.S.

7 Suki is an Asian elephant who will spend the rest of her life at "an elephant-prison" for "bad" elephants near Seattle in Washington state. *8* Since she is a killer and weighs over 2,000 pounds (1,000 kilograms), her handlers treat her very carefully. *9* When the handlers care for her, special movable walls act as "separators" between her and them. *10* Suki has two elephant-roommates who also are dangerous. *11* If their behavior improved, the three elephants could leave this elephant-prison. *12* However, no one expects that to happen.

13 In Suki's younger days as a circus performer, she was a good elephant. *14* Because she was very smart, she learned tricks easily. *15* Unfortunately, one of the tricks that she learned was a headstand. *16* One day, she did a headstand on one of her handlers and killed him. *17* Some time later, she killed a second handler in the same way. *18* After Suki tried to do a headstand on a third handler, she was finally sent to "the prison" for bad elephants. *19* Although her owners were disappointed that she could not perform with the circus any more, they were relieved to find "a home" for her.

sentences starting with the subject	sentences *not* starting with the subject
1	1 ✔
2	2
3	3
4	4
5	5
6	6
7	7
8	8
9	9
10	10
11	11
12	12
13	13
14	14
15	15
16	16
17	17
18	18
19	19

Exercise 3:

Practice using a variety of sentence styles.

❶. As a model, use the essay *"A Bad Elephant"* Text 2 (interesting style) on page 99.

❷. Rewrite the sentences below using the style in Text 2.

	In Text 2 (page 99), look at these sentences.
a. Everyone knows that chocolate is a favorite treat around the world. *Needless to say, chocolate is a favorite treat around the world.*	1
b. It is unfortunate that the future of chocolate is at risk.	15
c. Chocolate-producing companies must change their procedure if they want to prevent their cacao trees from dying at a rapid pace.	11
d. Cacao trees grow under taller trees in the rain forest.	4
e. They grow under trees which are taller because they need a lot of shade.	14
f. The chocolate-producing companies cut down big areas of the rain forest when they want to plant new cacao orchards.	9

g. The cacao trees then suffer from disease and insects because of a lack of shade.

2

_____

_____

_____

h. The trees produce fewer and less tasty beans after they get sick.

18

_____

_____

_____

i. Cacao trees lived a long time, some years ago, when they grew in their natural shady conditions.

17

_____

_____

_____

j. The chocolate companies now quickly abandon the sick orchards although the trees are still young.

19

_____

_____

_____

k. The companies then cut down more and more rain forest since they continually need space to plant new orchards.

8

_____

_____

_____

l. It is sad that these companies and their shortsighted methods are destroying rain forests and risking the future of chocolate.

15

_____

_____

_____

Grammar: *For practice with* **Wish** *and* **Hope***, do Grammar Unit 7.*

Strategy 7   Avoid repeating words and phrases.

Exercise 1: Underline the words and phrases that are repeated.

1. Tony bought a <u>dog that was big</u>. The <u>dog that was big</u> became a huge expense because the <u>dog</u> ate a lot of food.

2. After moving into our new apartment, we needed to shop for many items. First, we bought dishes for the kitchen, and we bought a used TV. After that, we bought a sofa. Last, we bought a lamp.

3. A person who has a problem with a computer often gets frustrated. The best thing that the person who has a problem with a computer can do is to take a break and forget about the computer for a few hours.

Exercise 2: Write the replacement words from these boxes over the underlined words to improve the style.

> - enjoyed _ • do this __ • there __ • it **X** • participated in __

1. We talked about the test. We knew that <u>the test</u> *it* would be hard. After discussing <u>the test</u>, *it* we began to study for the test.

2. To score more points in basketball, we need to practice shooting. If we <u>practice shooting</u>, our accuracy will improve.

3. I asked her why she had to go to the hospital. She said that she had gone <u>to the hospital</u> because she had cut her finger.

4. I had an active weekend. First, I played tennis. Next, I <u>played</u> video games with my nephew. After that, I <u>played</u> a card game with my parents.

> - them __ • they __ • They __ • ones __ • (take out the words) __ • She __

5. Travelers who are not careful sometimes have problems on a trip. <u>These travelers who are not careful</u> need to learn some techniques that <u>these travelers</u> can use to avoid trouble.

6. Jane got very excited in the fall when the leaves turned colors. <u>Jane</u> often spent several hours every day taking pictures of <u>the leaves</u> and collecting the colorful <u>leaves</u>.

7. Students who are not good in school usually do not pay attention in class. <u>These students who are not good in school</u> tend to whisper to their classmates during the lessons.

Exercise 3:

Improve the style of these sentences by changing or taking out repeated words.

1. The life of fishermen has its good and bad points. The fishermen have a lot of freedom and the fishermen get to work outside. However, experiencing storms at sea must be scary for the fishermen.

2. My friend took a trip to Africa. During his travels, he was able to photograph several wild animals. Unfortunately, he didn't see any lions in Africa.

3. Ken stood in line all night in order to get good seats for the concert. Because he had stood in line all night, he was able to sit close enough to the performers to get autographs.

4. My sister had twins (two babies born on the same day), but because the twins were so tiny when the twins were born, the doctors decided to keep the twins in the hospital for three weeks. Because twins are rare, a lot of visitors came to see the twins.

5. Small towns have low buildings, and big cities have tall buildings.

6. During the meeting, Dan's cell phone rang several times. Finally, he decided that he had better turn the cell phone off.

7. Tim wanted to change his appearance. To change his appearance, he dyed his hair blond.

8. My father recently retired from his job in a factory. He had worked at the factory for over 45 years.

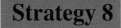

Strategy 8   Get a reaction from a peer.

Exercise 1:

❶. Imagine that you have a classmate, Jim, who wants your opinion about this first draft of his essay, *"Airplane Seatmates."*

❷. Read Jim's essay below but ignore his mistakes.

Airplane Seatmates

During a plane long flight, it's important to find some pleasant ways to pass the time. Because I was planning to take a 12-hour flight overseas, I decided that I wanted a seatmate (in other words, the person sitting next to me on the flight) who could make the 12 hours as enjoyable as possible. I asked two people *1* several questions in order to help me choose which one I wanted as a seatmate.

2 Ken is likes to talking. *3* He's had many unusual experiences, so he talks about his unusual experiences. For example, three years ago, he climbed the highest mountain in the world. He also hiked across the Sahara Desert. *4* Also, a plane that he was on was hijacked. *5* Also, he has an opinion about everything. If someone mentions sports, politics, cars, movies, or even the weather, Ken wants to say what he thinks. He once talked for an hour about which cities had the best Chinese food. *6* Ken is talkative, Ann is quiet. This doesn't mean that she never speaks. She has visited several interesting places like Brazil and Thailand, but she seldom talks about them. *7* She seems more interested in listening than talking. She often will ask a short but excellent question to learn about the other person. For example, I told her that I was thinking about quitting my job because of all the problems that I was having with my boss. She listened to my complaints silently and then asked me if I had told my boss how I felt. Actually, I hadn't, but I then decided that I should try that.

On an airplane, I sometimes feel uncomfortable because the seats are small. I need to spread out my legs and arms if possible. Ken is a big, 30-year-old fellow. *8* Ken is about 6 feet, 4 inches tall and weighs about 230 pounds. When he is sitting down, it looks like he needs two seats. *9* Ann is small. Some people think that she is a teenager because she is so tiny, even though she is almost 40 years old. She told me an interesting story about her size. One day, she was at a shopping mall with her 16-year-old daughter. While they were looking at some clothes, a couple of teenage boys started a conversation with them. After a few minutes, they invited Ann and her daughter to a party. Ann didn't want to embarrass the boys, so she just told them that her mother wouldn't let her stay out after 10 p.m.

Finally, for me, one of the pleasures of traveling by plane is the food. Surprisingly, both *10* Ann and Ken like the food served on planes, too. However, I imagine that Ann would not eat all of her meal; in other words, she would probably share her dessert with me. Unlike Ann, Ken would probably *11* ate all of his food and even ask me for some of *12* mine.

I am not looking forward to *13* sit on an airplane for 12 hours. *14* Because I tend to get bored after 30 minutes. I always need something to distract me. As a result, I have decided to choose Ken as my seatmate.

Although we will feel crowded sitting next to each other and although I might have to give him some of my dinner, I don't think I will mind it, because he will probably entertain me with all of his stories and opinions. I think that *15* I and Ken will have a great time together. *16*

Exercise 2:

Imagine that Jim asks you these questions about the essay above. Write your advice.

A. Look where I marked 1. Should I tell their names here?

B. Look at the underlined sentence after 2. Is there something wrong with it? If so, how can I fix it?

C. Look at the sentence after 3. How can I improve this sentence so that I don't repeat the words "unusual experiences?"

D. Look at 4 and 5. I've repeated the word "also." How can I avoid this?

E. I know that there is a grammar problem with the sentence after 6. How can I fix it?

F. Look at 7. Would it be helpful if I wrote "Unlike Ken" before the word "she?"

G. In the 2 sentences before and after 8, I repeated the word "Ken." How can I avoid this?

H. At the start of 9, what expression describing differences (from page 77) should I put here?

I. Do you see where I marked 10? Does it matter whether I say "Ann and Ken" or "Ken and Ann?"

J. At 11, is "ate" the correct verb tense here? Why (not)?

K. At 12, should I keep the word "mine" or change it to "my food?"

L. At 13, is the word "sit" correct here or should it be "sat" or "sitting?"

M. In the underlined sentence after 14, how can I correct the grammar problem?

N. For 15, does it matter whether I say "I and Ken" or "Ken and I?"

O. For 16, in my conclusion, do you think that I explained my decision clearly?

Exercise 3:

(Optional) Before preparing questions to ask a classmate about your own essay, write another draft of the essay that you wrote on page 91. Try to:

- add details and examples,
- use a variety of sentence styles,
- change words so that you don't repeat them.

Exercise 4:

Use the draft of the essay that you wrote.

❶. Write some numbers on the essay in places where you would like some advice from another student. (See samples on page 105.)
❷. On a different paper, write some questions that you would like to ask. (See samples below.)

Possible questions that you might ask to get advice

- Do you think that I need more details here?
- Can you understand this sentence?
- How can I combine these two sentences?
- Is this part interesting?
- Can you help me think of some details that I could put here?
- Do you think that there is a grammar problem in this sentence?
- How can I avoid repeating this word?
- Should I add an example here?

Exercise 5:

❶. Exchange papers with a classmate.
❷. Silently read your classmate's essay.
❸. Point to places on your essay where you would like advice and ask your questions.
   (Just discuss your advice. You do not have to write your advice.)
   (You do not have to make any changes to your essay if you do not want to.)
❹. Also, answer your classmate's questions about their essay.

Exercise 6:

(Optional) Interview the two people again that you had interviewed for your essay. Ask questions to get more information, examples, and details.

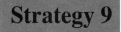

Strategy 9   Improve the sentence style and vocabulary on your final draft.

Exercise 1:

Fill in the blanks with the correct words from the box. These are replacements for the underlined words in the essay.

Paragraph 1:

- decide which one I wanted to work for ___   • college, he ___   • Because I know ___
- After my **✗**   • graduating, but my ___   • well, many ___   • it ___

Paragraph 2:

- employers, Mr. Tanner and Mr. Olsen, ___   • he ___
- about my interest in hiking and dogs ___   • not only as ___   • but also as ___
- Unlike Mr. Tanner, Mr. Olsen ___   • know about me as a person ___

Paragraph 3:

- aspect ___   • Likewise, Mr. Olsen ___   • him ___
- In contrast to Mr. Tanner, Mr. Olsen said ___   • carefully follow ___
- By this I mean what ___

Paragraph 4:

- Mercedes and Rolls Royces ___   • luxurious house ___   • He ___
- The reason for this was that he ___

Paragraph 5:

- friend since he ___   • would benefit from ___
- However, Mr. Tanner ___   • After careful consideration, I decided ___

Comparing Two Employers

After my

1 ∆ M̶y̶ father finished ∆ college. He spent a long time looking for a job. Finally, he was offered a job, and he immediately took ∆ the job. Now I am ∆ graduating. My situation is quite different from his. ∆ *I know* computers so ∆ well, so many companies want to hire me. There are two companies that I am interested in, so I decided to interview the employees at both places in order to help me ∆ decide which is better.

---

2 For me, most important is a boss who seems interested in me as an employee and as a person. Both employers seemed interested in me as an employee. Mr. Tanner often looked me in the eyes and asked me about my life outside of work. After we talked about my work experience and educational background, Mr. Tanner wanted to know about me. For example, we talked about what I enjoy. On the other hand, Mr. Olsen only nodded his head when I talked about these. Mr. Olsen quickly changed the topic back to my work and skills.

3 Another thing about an employer that I am concerned about is his expectations of me. What he wants me to do, when he wants me to do it, and how he wants it done. Mr. Tanner carefully explained my job duties. Mr. Olsen told me what he expected of me. There was a difference between them, though Mr. Tanner wanted me to follow his guidelines. Also, with Mr. Tanner, I would have an 8 a.m. to 5 p.m. schedule and would have to work in an assigned office. Mr. Olsen said that I would have a lot of freedom in my job. Mr. Olsen said that I could choose my work hours and where I wanted to work.

4 Finally, I considered how successful these two men were. Mr. Tanner seemed to be successful. Mr. Tanner smiled and told me about his big house, his fancy cars, his expensive vacations and his African butterfly collection. On the other hand, Mr. Olsen had a huge house, too, but he rarely took a vacation. He was too busy at work.

5 I decided to take the job with Mr. Tanner. I feel that both men are successful. Mr. Tanner seemed like the type of boss who could become almost a good friend. He wanted to know what I liked to do outside of work. Also, although Mr. Olsen would give me freedom at work, I think that, as a new employee, I would like the structure that Mr. Tanner could give me.

Exercise 2:

Write a final draft of your essay.

❶. Try to improve the sentence style and vocabulary.

❷. Include some of the suggestions that your classmate gave you in the exercise on page 106, if they were useful.

Grammar: *For practice with* **Starting Sentences with Dependent Clauses**, *do Grammar Unit 30.*

Teachers: see the Teacher's Manual for photocopyable:

- Comparison and Contrast Check-list
- Comparison and Contrast Evaluation Form
- In-class Essay Topics for Comparison and Contrast

Section 2: Fluency Writing

A

Fluency Writing 1

DO NOT LOOK AT YOUR PARTNERS' PAGES.

Before Step 1:

   1. Silently read the article below.

   2. Write answers to the comprehension questions below.

A Boy Is Burned
While Trying to Copy a TV Stuntman (part 1)

TV is a powerful force nowadays, especially in the lives of young people who may believe that things which they see on TV are real. ***Did you understand what I just said?*** A 13-year-old boy living near Seattle learned a tough lesson about the difference between real life and the images on TV.

The boy had seen stuntmen on TV who could do crazy and dangerous things and then walk away perfectly fine. ***Understand?*** One day, the boy and his two friends were playing, and he asked the friends to help set him on fire. To do this, first, the friends (who were 13- and 14 years old) sprayed the boy with a certain chemical, called WD 40, which is popular for treating rusty metal. But when they lit the match and tried to start the boy on fire, it failed to work. ***Got it?***

Step 1:

   1. Read your article to your partners. If they don't understand something, explain with different words.

   2. Ask your partners these comprehension questions.

Comprehension Questions

   1. How old was the boy?

   2. What did the stuntmen on TV do?

   3. What did the boy want his friends to help him do?

   4. What did they do with the WD 40? Why?

Steps 2 & 3:

   1. Listen to your partners read the next parts of the article. If you don't understand something, ask them to explain in different words.

   2. Answer their comprehension questions.

Step 4: Do the exercise on page 115.

Fluency Writing 1

DO NOT LOOK AT YOUR PARTNERS' PAGES.

Before Step 1:

1. Silently read the article below.
2. Write answers to the comprehension questions below.

A Boy Is Burned
While Trying to Copy a TV Stuntman (part 2)

This is the second part of the article.

Next, the friends sprayed the boy with charcoal lighter-fluid, which is a popular chemical for starting outdoor grills. They lit a match, but it failed to work. **Did you understand?**

Finally, they got some hair spray and sprayed the boy with it from head to toe. Then, they lit another match and, this time, it worked! The boy caught fire! He quickly dropped to the floor and rolled around, just as he had seen the stuntmen do on TV, and the flames went out. **Got it?**

Since the trick was a success, the boys tried it again. They added more hair spray and charcoal lighter-fluid and set the boy on fire again. He dropped and rolled but, this time, there were too many chemicals, and the flames would not go out! Immediately, the friends called 911, the emergency phone number. **Should I explain that again?**

Step 1:

1. Listen to Student A read the first part of the article. If you don't understand something, ask them to explain in different words.
2. Answer their comprehension questions.

Step 2:

1. Read your article to your partners. If they don't understand something, explain with different words.
2. Ask your partners these comprehension questions.

Comprehension Questions

1. What did the friends do with the charcoal-lighter fluid?
2. What happened when they lit the match?
3. What did they spray on the boy next?
4. Did the hairspray work?
5. What did the boy do the first time he caught fire?
6. What happened the second time he caught fire?

Step 3:

1. Listen to Student C read the last part of the article. If you don't understand something, ask them to explain in different words.
2. Answer their comprehension questions.

Step 4: Do the exercise on page 115.

Fluency Writing 1

Before Step 1:

1. Silently read the article below.
2. Write answers to the comprehension questions below.

A Boy Is Burned
While Trying to Copy a TV Stuntman (part 3)

This is the third part of the article.

When the firemen arrived, they put out the flames and asked the friends what had happened. *Understand?* The friends lied and said that they were not doing anything dangerous. However, the fire chief was suspicious, so he smelled the boy's clothes. He noticed a strong smell of lighter-fluid and questioned the boys' original explanation. A few minutes later, the friends decided to tell the truth. *OK?*

In the end, the injured boy was taken by helicopter to the hospital. After considering the case, the police decided not to arrest the friends because the original idea had come from the boy who was burned. *Did you understand what I said?*

This true story should remind parents and teachers that young people (not only 5-or 6-year olds, but also, 13- and 14-year olds) can confuse reality with the images that they see on TV. Adults need to make sure that young people understand the difference. *Do you want me to explain that again?*

Step 1 & 2:

1. Listen to your partners read the first parts of the article. If you don't understand something, ask them to explain in different words.
2. Answer their comprehension questions.

Step 3:

1. Read your article to your partners. If they don't understand something, explain with different words.
2. Ask your partners these comprehension questions.

Comprehension Questions

1. At first, did the boys tell the truth to the firemen about what happened?

2. Why was the fire chief suspicious?

3. Did the injured boy stay home the rest of the day?

4. Why do some young people do things that they see on TV?

Step 4: Do the exercise on page 115.

Fluency Writing 1

DO NOT look at the article again. You can ask your partners to give you some details again if you want.

Students

A, B, & C

Step 4: Fluency Writing Exercise

1. Write a paragraph with as many details as you can about "Boy is Burned."
   You can use the "Key Words and Phrases" to write your paper.
2. Write about the information from **all three parts of the article** (Part 1, Part 2 and Part 3), not just your part.

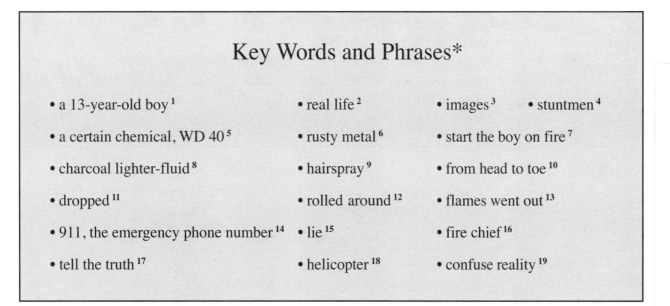

Key Words and Phrases*

- a 13-year-old boy [1]
- a certain chemical, WD 40 [5]
- charcoal lighter-fluid [8]
- dropped [11]
- 911, the emergency phone number [14]
- tell the truth [17]

- real life [2]
- rusty metal [6]
- hairspray [9]
- rolled around [12]
- lie [15]
- helicopter [18]

- images [3] • stuntmen [4]
- start the boy on fire [7]
- from head to toe [10]
- flames went out [13]
- fire chief [16]
- confuse reality [19]

* The numbers with the key words and phrases indicate the order in which they appear in the story.

A

Fluency Writing 2

DO NOT LOOK AT YOUR PARTNERS' PAGES.

Before Step 1:

1. Silently read the article below.
2. Write answers to the comprehension questions below.

Grizzly Bear (part 1)

Almost every night, 70-year-old Ken Larson has the same nightmare. In it, he is trying to escape, but he can't. Then he wakes up and feels relieved to see that he is still in his hospital room. ***Did you understand that?***

In early June of 1999, he was staying at a hotel near Glacier National Park in Montana. Early in the morning of June 5th, he left the hotel to take a 4-mile hike. Most guests at the hotel were still asleep when he started out on a trail. ***Understand?*** Soon, he came to a sign that said, "Grizzly Country: Be careful." Larson ignored the sign and continued his hike. He had read that hikers should make noise so that they don't surprise a grizzly. As a result, he regularly called out, "HELLO." ***Got it?***

Suddenly, he saw a grizzly coming around a corner in front of him. The bear began to run toward him with its mouth wide open.

"Oh, my God!" Larson shouted. "He's going to get me!"

He jumped off the trail and tried to hide in some bushes. The bear followed Larson into the bushes and hit Larson's head. Its claws cut a big wound across the back of the head. ***OK?***

Step 1:

1. Read your article to your partner. If they don't understand something, explain with different words.
2. Ask your partner these comprehension questions.

Comprehension Questions

1. Where is Ken Larson now?
2. Why did he get up early on the morning of June 5th, 1999?
3. What did the sign on the trail say?
4. Why did he call out "Hello?"
5. What did the bear do to Larson?

Step 2:

1. Listen to your partner read the second part of the article. If you don't understand something, ask them to explain in different words.
2. Answer their comprehension questions.

Step 3: Do the exercise on page 118.

Fluency Writing 2

DO NOT LOOK AT YOUR PARTNERS' PAGES.

Before Step 1:
1. Silently read the article below.
2. Write answers to the comprehension questions below.

Grizzly Bear (part 2)

This is the second part of the article.

Ken Larson had read that if a grizzly attacks, we should pretend that we are dead, so he curled up in a ball on the ground. However, the bear continued to attack. Larson could feel the bear's claws and teeth on his neck, shoulders and stomach. He realized that he was probably going to die. He moaned in pain, but he didn't scream. ***Do you understand?***

The bear made one last big attack. He bit Larson's leg and broke it. The whole attack lasted only 30 seconds.

Although his leg was broken, Larson was able to crawl down the trail. Two park workers found him and took him to a hospital by helicopter. ***OK?***

The park rangers said that Larson had made some terrible mistakes that day. First, he was hiking alone. Also, walking in the early morning was a dangerous time of day. Third, he probably wasn't making enough noise. ***Got it?***

A lot of tourists at Glacier National Park worry about bear attacks, but, surprisingly, bear attacks are actually very rare. In fact, tourists are more likely to drown in a lake or fall off a cliff than to die from a grizzly bear attack. ***Understand?***

Step 1:
1. Listen to your partner read the first part of the article. If you don't understand something, ask them to explain in different words.
2. Answer their comprehension questions.

Step 2:
1. Read your article to your partner. If they don't understand something, explain with different words.
2. Ask your partner these comprehension questions.

Comprehension Questions
1. In general, what should a hiker do if a bear attacks?
2. Where on Ken Larson's body did the bear hurt him?
3. How long did the bear attack last?
4. What three things did Larson do wrong?
5. Which is more likely to happen to a tourist: get killed by a bear or drown in a lake?

Step 3: Do the exercise on page 118.

Fluency Writing 2

Students

A & B

Step 4: Fluency Writing Exercise

1. Write a paragraph with as many details as you can about the article "Grizzly Bear."
   You can use the "Key Words and Phrases" to write your paper.
2. Write about the information from **both parts of the article** (Part 1 and Part 2),
   not just your part.

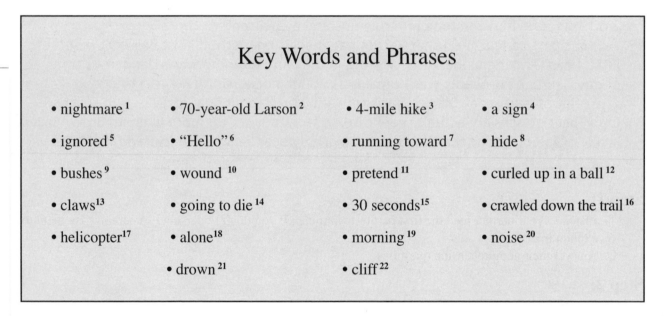

Key Words and Phrases

- nightmare [1]
- 70-year-old Larson [2]
- 4-mile hike [3]
- a sign [4]

- ignored [5]
- "Hello" [6]
- running toward [7]
- hide [8]

- bushes [9]
- wound [10]
- pretend [11]
- curled up in a ball [12]

- claws [13]
- going to die [14]
- 30 seconds [15]
- crawled down the trail [16]

- helicopter [17]
- alone [18]
- morning [19]
- noise [20]

- drown [21]
- cliff [22]

Fluency Writing 3

DO NOT LOOK AT YOUR PARTNERS' PAGES.

Before Step 1:
1. Silently read the article below.
2. Write answers to the comprehension questions below.

Cheating at School (part 1)

A questionnaire asked college students all over the United States about cheating. Surprisingly, 90% of the students said that cheating is wrong, but more than 70% said they had cheated in high school anyway. ***Did you understand?*** This surprisingly high percentage of cheaters raises questions, such as: Why is cheating so common? What type of student is actually doing the cheating? And, how should parents handle a child who cheats?

The responses which 6,000 college students gave on the questionnaire helped answer some of those questions. For example, it found that most college students cheated because of pressure to get good grades. ***Got it?*** The research also found that more males than females cheat. Also, students at larger state universities are more likely to cheat than those at smaller colleges.

Actually, for very young children, cheating is quite rare. Perhaps the main reason for this is that, in order to cheat, a child needs to have the basic skills of reading and writing. ***Do you want me to explain any of that again?***

Step 1:
1. Read your article to your partners. If they don't understand something, explain with different words.
2. Ask your partners these comprehension questions.

Comprehension Questions

1. What percent of college students said that cheating is wrong?
2. What percent of college students said that they had cheated in high school?
3. Who cheats more: males or females?
4. Where do more students cheat: at large universities or small colleges?
5. Is it common or rare for young children to cheat?
6. What do young children need in order to cheat?

Steps 2 & 3:
1. Listen to your partners read the next parts of the article. If you don't understand something, ask them to explain in different words.
2. Answer their comprehension questions.

Step 4: Do the exercise on page 122.

Fluency Writing 3

DO NOT LOOK AT YOUR PARTNERS' PAGES.

Before Step 1:
1. Silently read the article below.
2. Write answers to the comprehension questions below.

Cheating at School (part 2)

This is the second part of the article.

As (Student A) said, it is quite rare for young children to cheat. However, some youngsters cheat because they really do not understand that it is wrong. They just find that it is a convenient way to get better grades. **Did you understand?** However, parents who have a child who is cheating need to realize that the child is sending them a message. The message is that the child is having problems in school.

During high school years, the cases of cheating increase greatly. Some high school students cheat because they have trouble meeting the expectations of parents, teachers and themselves. **Do you understand the word "expectations"?** For those students, cheating is an easy solution to a difficult problem.

Many parents have no idea about how to deal with a son or daughter who cheats. Most parents believe that cheating is more serious than other discipline problems, like fighting. This may be true because it is quite easy to know if a child is fighting, since they will have physical signs, like bruises or torn clothes, but cheating has few obvious signs, unless teachers report it to parents. **Got it?**

Step 1:

Listen to Student A read the first part of the article. If you don't understand something, ask them to explain in different words. Answer their comprehension questions.

Step 2:
1. Read your article to your partners. If they don't understand something, explain with different words.
2. Ask your partners these comprehension questions.

Comprehension Questions
1. What is the reason some young children cheat?
2. What message are children who cheat sending to their parents?
3. Does cheating increase or decrease during high school years?
4. Why do some high school students cheat?
5. Which do parents consider more serious: cheating or fighting?
6. Why is it more difficult for parents to know if their child is cheating than if he is fighting?

Step 3:

Listen to Student C read the last part of the article. If you don't understand something, ask them to explain in different words. Answer their comprehension questions.

Step 4: Do the exercise on page 122.

Fluency Writing 3

DO NOT LOOK AT YOUR PARTNERS' PAGES.

Before Step 1:

1. Silently read the article below.
2. Write answers to the comprehension questions below.

Cheating at School (part 3)

This is the third part of the article.

There are a few things that parents can do about cheating. First, they should analyze whether they are good role models for their children. *Do you understand "role models"?* Young people often get "mixed signals" from parents concerning honesty and cheating. For example, young people might overhear their parents talking about not telling a store clerk when they are given back too much change for a purchase, or teenagers might notice that their parents try to pay cheaper "children's prices" for their movie ticket, because a teenager's ticket is more expensive. *OK?* From bad parental examples such as these, children will learn that it is acceptable to use any technique possible to get what they want.

Parents should also realize that just getting angry and punishing a child for cheating is seldom helpful. If parents get angry, the child will probably feel even more pressure to get good grades. This might cause him to cheat even more. *Got it?* Instead, parents should explain that cheating is wrong and help him develop good study habits so that he can do his school-work honestly in the future. *Understand?*

Step 1 & 2:

1. Listen to your partners read the first parts of the article. If you don't understand something, ask them to explain in different words.
2. Answer their comprehension questions.

Step 3:

1. Read your article to your partners. If they don't understand something, explain with different words.
2. Ask your partners these comprehension questions.

Comprehension Questions

1. What should parents be for their children?
2. In a short answer, explain what the expression "mixed signals" means.
3. What is an example of a mixed signal that parents give their children?
4. Should parents get angry at a child who cheats?
3. Why or why not?
4. What should parents do if their child cheats?

Step 4: Do the exercise on page 122.

Fluency Writing 3

DO NOT look at the article again. You can ask your partners to give you some details again if you want.

Students
A, B, & C

Step 4: Fluency Writing Exercise

1. Write a paragraph with as many details as you can about "Cheating in School."
   You can use the "Key Words and Phrases" to write your paper.
2. Write about the information from **all three parts of the article** (Part 1, Part 2 and Part 3),
   not just your part.

Key Words and Phrases

- a questionnaire asked[1]

- 6,000 college students[3]

- males / females[5]

- young children[7]

- reason for cheating: children[9]

- reason for cheating: high school students[11]

- fighting / cheating[13]

- role models[15]

- get angry[17]

- more pressure[19]

- 90% / 70%[2]

- reason for cheating: college students[4]

- small colleges / large universities[6]

- basic skills[8]

- send a message[10]

- parents[12]

- bruises[14]

- mixed signals[16]

- punish[18]

- study habits[20]

Fluency Writing 4

DO NOT LOOK AT YOUR PARTNERS' PAGES.

Before Step 1:

1. Silently read the article below.
2. Write answers to the comprehension questions below.

Police Dogs (part 1)

Today, there are about 8,000 police dogs working in the U.S. The police use them to catch criminals, like robbers, murderers, and drug dealers. They are also used to find lost children or patients with mental problems who have walked away from home. *Do you understand?*

Police officers and their police dogs get the most dangerous assignments. They usually work during the night shift, when it is "high crime time." Often, when the police are trying to arrest a criminal, just the presence of a police dog can make a difference. Criminals who are chased by a police dog usually give up without a fight. As a result, the typical police dog bites only about one criminal a year. *Got it?*

Most police dogs are German shepherds because of their controlled temperament. When they are not working, a policeman and his dog eat, sleep and live together. When they are on duty, they respect each other and work like a team. A good police dog needs to be vicious when chasing a criminal but gentle when dealing with a child. When a dog finds a human, it will look at the officer to find out what to do. If the officer looks happy because they found a lost child, the dog will not bark or attack. But, if the officer looks nervous because they found a criminal, the dog will bark angrily and perhaps try to bite the person. *Understand?*

Step 1:

1. Read your article to your partner. If they don't understand something, explain with different words.
2. Ask your partner these comprehension questions.

Comprehension Questions

1. What kinds of jobs are police dogs used for?
2. Do criminals usually fight or give up when they are chased by a police dog?
3. Where do the police dogs live when they are not working?
4. On average, how often do they bite a criminal?
5. Why must police dogs have a controlled temperament?

Step 2:

1. Listen to your partner read the second part of the article. If you don't understand something, ask them to explain in different words.
2. Answer their comprehension questions.

Step 3: Do the exercise on page 125.

Fluency Writing 4

Before Step 1:
1. Silently read the article below.
2. Write answers to the comprehension questions below.

Police Dogs (part 2)

This is the second part of the article.

Police dogs actually enjoy their work, and the police officers try to make it as fun for them as possible. In fact, before going on a drug search, an officer will say to his dog, "Do you want to play?" That helps the dog get excited and focused. *Got it?*

Criminals who are escaping from a dog sometimes take off their shirt and throw it away in order to confuse the dog. However, this is a waste of time. Dogs follow the smell of a human being himself, not his clothes. If a robber is running through a shopping mall, a police dog will not be able to smell him, because there are too many other people around. But if the criminal is hiding in a huge, empty forest, the dog will be able to smell him quite easily. *Do you want me to explain that again?*

On average, a police dog works for about seven years. After he retires, he may continue to live with the policeman who had been his partner at work. *OK?*

Step 1:
1. Listen to your partner read the first part of the article. If you don't understand something, ask them to explain in different words.
2. Answer their comprehension questions.

Step 2:
1. Read your article to your partner. If they don't understand something, explain with different words.
2. Ask your partner these comprehension questions.

Comprehension Questions

1. What does a police officer say to his dog before going on a drug search?

   Why does he say this?

2. Explain why it is a waste of time for a convict to take off his shirt in order

   to confuse the dog?

3. Where can a dog easily smell a particular person: in a shopping mall or an empty forest?

4. How many years does a typical police dog work?

5. Where does the dog often live after he retires?

Step 3: Do the exercise on page 125.

Fluency Writing 4

Students
A & B

Step 4: Fluency Writing Exercise

1. Write a paragraph with as many details as you can about "Police Dogs."
   You can use the "Key Words and Phrases" to write your paper.
2. Write about the information from **both parts of the article** (Part 1 and Part 2),
   not just your part.

Key Words and Phrases

- 8,000 [1]
- lost children [3]
- night shift [5]
- give up without a fight [7]
- vicious / gentle [9]
- bark [11]
- excited and focused [13]
- follow the smell of a human being [15]
- empty forest [17]
- retires [19]

- criminals [2]
- patients with mental problems [4]
- arrest [6]
- controlled temperament [8]
- look happy / nervous [10]
- enjoy [12]
- take off their shirt [14]
- shopping mall [16]
- seven years [18]

Fluency Writing 5

DO NOT LOOK AT YOUR PARTNERS' PAGES.

Before Step 1:

1. Silently read the article below.
2. Write answers to the comprehension questions below.

Music Therapy (part 1)

This article explains how music can be used to help people with physical and mental problems. ***Do you understand?***

Here is one example. An elderly woman was in a nursing home. ***Do you understand what a nursing home is?***

This woman had not spoken any words in several months. One day, she was sitting in a room, and someone nearby began playing a song on a piano. Soon the elderly woman began humming the song. ***Understand?***

A few minutes later, she started talking very clearly with her relatives who were sitting near her. Everyone was astonished. ***Got it?***

Here is a second example of how music has helped someone. There was a mentally-disturbed young man who was in a mental hospital because he had committed a number of serious crimes. ***OK?***

While in the hospital, he learned how to play the guitar. Within a few months, he organized a band and started writing his own music. Also, he began to socialize more with other people. He has improved so much that he may soon be released from the hospital. ***Understand?***

Step 1:

1. Read your article to your partners. If they don't understand something, explain with different words.
2. Ask your partners these comprehension questions.

Comprehension Questions

1. In the first example, where did the elderly woman live?

2. What was the first thing that she did when someone started playing the piano?

3. Why was everyone astonished?

4. In the second example, why was the young man in a mental hospital?

5. How did music change this man?

Steps 2 & 3:

1. Listen to your partners read the next parts of the article. If you don't understand something, ask them to explain in different words.
2. Answer their comprehension questions.

Step 4: Do the exercise on page 129.

Fluency Writing 5

DO NOT LOOK AT YOUR PARTNERS' PAGES.

Before Step 1:

1. Silently read the article below.
2. Write answers to the comprehension questions below.

Music Therapy (part 2)

This is the second part of the article.

Music has helped patients in dentist offices. One patient needed some painful work done on this teeth. Unfortunately, he could not take any painkillers because he was very sensitive to medication. *Understand so far?*

So, instead, the dentist gave him stereo headphones, and he listened to his favorite music while the dentist worked on his teeth. He hardly felt any pain. *Got it?*

Dentist offices, nursing homes for the elderly and mental hospitals are three places where music can help patients. There is a field of study called "Music Therapy," in which music is used to help cure people with problems like brain disease, drug addictions, and stress. It even can help mothers during child birth. *Understand?*

Step 1:

1. Listen to Student A read the first part of the article. If you don't understand something, ask them to explain in different words.
2. Answer their comprehension questions.

Step 2:

1. Read your article to your partners. If they don't understand something, explain with different words.
2. Ask your partners these comprehension questions.

Comprehension Questions

1. Why couldn't the dental patient take any painkillers?
2. What was the effect of listening to music for the patient?
3. What is the field of study which is discussed?
4. Tell me at least three types of problems which music can help to cure.

Step 3:

1. Listen to Student C read the last part of the article. If you don't understand something, ask them to explain in different words.
2. Answer their Comprehension Questions.

Step 4: Do the exercise on page 129.

Student

Fluency Writing 5

Before Step 1:

1. Silently read the article below.

2. Write answers to the comprehension questions below.

Music Therapy (part 3)

This is the third part of the article.

Today, more than 70 colleges offer programs in music therapy. A person who completes the program is called a music therapist. *Understand?*

Music therapists work in many places, such as mental hospitals, drug and alcohol recovery centers, nursing homes, prisons, and schools. *Got it?*

There are several ways that therapists use music. The simplest way is to let patients just listen to music on an instrument or stereo. Another way is to encourage patients to participate by singing or tapping a small drum along with the music. A third way is to actually let patients play an instrument. Finally, a more advanced way is to have patients learn to write music. *OK?*

One of the most exciting results takes place when patients organize a band. This group activity is very important for patients who have problems socializing with others. *Understand?*

Step 1 & 2:

1. Listen to your partners read the first parts of the article. If you don't understand something, ask them to explain in different words.

2. Answer their comprehension questions.

Step 3:

1. Read your article to your partners. If they don't understand something, explain with different words.

2. Ask your partners these comprehension questions.

Comprehension Questions

1. How many colleges offer programs in music therapy nowadays?

2. What do we call a person who completes this type of program?

3. What is the simplest way that therapists use music?

4. What are other ways?

5. What kind of patient benefits most from playing in a band?

Step 4: Do the exercise on page 129.

Fluency Writing 5

Students

A, B, & C

Step 4: Fluency Writing Exercise

1. Write a paragraph with as many details as you can about "Music Therapy."
    You can use the "Key Words and Phrases" to write your paper.
2. Write about the information from **all three parts of the article** (Part 1, Part 2 and Part 3), not just your part.

Key Words and Phrases

- elderly woman in a nursing home [1]
- humming the song [3]
- mentally disturbed [5]
- committed crimes [7]
- band [9]
- dentist's office [11]
- pain-killers [13]
- headphones [15]
- hardly felt any pain [17]
- college programs [19]
- several ways that therapists use music [21]
- write music [23]

- piano [2]
- astonished [4]
- a mental hospital [6]
- guitar [8]
- socialize [10]
- needed work done [12]
- sensitive to medication [14]
- have trouble socializing [16]
- cure people with problems [18]
- music therapists work in many places [20]
- The simplest way is to [22]
- bands [24]

Fluency Writing 6

DO NOT LOOK AT YOUR PARTNERS' PAGES.

Before Step 1:

1. Silently read the article below.
2. Write answers to the comprehension questions below.

Stopping a Drunk Driver (part 1)

Beverly Gentry is a 67-year-old grandmother. She is also an alcoholic. Over the years, she has driven a car while she was drunk hundreds of times. Thanks to a new invention called a Breathalyzer, Gentry's children no longer have to worry about her driving while she is drunk. The Breathalyzer is a device which is connected to the ignition of a car. **Do you understand so far?**

Here is how it works: First, drivers must blow into the device and, if their breath registers a 1.5 blood alcohol level, the car will not start. If the average person had between 3 and 7 drinks, the blood alcohol level would be 1.5. At this level, a driver is 25 times more likely to have a deadly car accident. **Got it?**

If the driver's breath is clean, the car will start. After several minutes, the driver must repeat the breath test while driving. By checking the drivers' breath often while they are driving, they will not be able to cheat; in other words, they will not be able to start the car and then start drinking. If drivers are unable to pass the test while they are driving, the car's horn will start beeping nonstop until the driver turns off the engine. **Do you want me to repeat that?**

Step 1:

1. Read your article to your partners. If they don't understand something, explain with different words.
2. Ask your partners these comprehension questions.

Comprehension Questions

1. What part of the car is the Breathalyzer connected to:

    (a) the gas pedal (b) the ignition (c) the steering wheel?

2. What does a 1.5 blood alcohol level mean?

3. How does a driver start a car if a Breathalyzer is connected to it?

4. What happens if a driver's blood alcohol level is over 1.5?

5. What happens after the car starts and the driver begins driving?

Steps 2 & 3:

1. Listen to your partners read the next parts of the article. If you don't understand something, ask them to explain in different words.
2. Answer their comprehension questions.

Step 4: Do the exercise on page 133.

Fluency Writing 6

DO NOT LOOK AT YOUR PARTNERS' PAGES.

Before Step 1:
1. Silently read the article below.
2. Write answers to the comprehension questions below.

Stopping a Drunk Driver (part 2)

This is the second part of the article.

In order to learn about the effectiveness of the Breathalyzer, researchers studied drivers who had repeated problems with drinking and driving. They found that drivers who used the device were 65% less likely to have another alcohol-related driving accident than those who did not use it. *Did you understand?*

Beverly Gentry has kept the Breathalyzer in her car for a decade. *Do you understand the word "decade"?* During this time, she has only driven while she was drunk once; it was a time when she beat the machine.

One day, Gentry planned to take her car to a repair-shop to have some repairs done. However, she knew that every time the mechanics started the car to move it or to work on the engine, they would have to blow into the device. This would take them a lot of extra time. *Got it?* As a result, Gentry asked her son-in-law, who was a police officer, to remove the device for the day. He agreed and Gentry took her car to the repair-shop for work. *Understand?*

Step 1:

Listen to Student A read the first part of the article. If you don't understand something, ask them to explain in different words. Answer their comprehension questions.

Step 2:

1. Read your article to your partners. If they don't understand something, explain with different words.
2. Ask your partners these comprehension questions.

Comprehension Questions

1. According to researchers, how effective is this device?
2. How many years has Gentry had the Breathalyzer?
3. How often has she been able to beat the machine?
4. Why would the device take extra time for the mechanics?
5. Who removed the device?

Step 3:

1. Listen to Student C read the last part of the article. If you don't understand something, ask them to explain in different words.
2. Answer their comprehension questions.

Step 4: Do the exercise on page 133.

Fluency Writing 6

C **Student**

Before Step 1:
1. Silently read the article below.
2. Write answers to the comprehension questions below.

Stopping a Drunk Driver (part 3)

This is the third part of the article.

Beverly Gentry picked up her car from the repair-shop and drove home. She had no plans to drive her car again for the rest of the day. However, she drank some alcohol which caused her to use poor judgment. After drinking, she drove to pick up some Chinese food and, on the way home, drove into a ditch and banged her head hard on the dashboard. She wasn't wearing a seatbelt. **Did you understand that?**

For two weeks, her son, daughter and three grandchildren visited her in the hospital. They were expecting her to die, but she recovered. After seeing the worried looks on her family members' faces, she promised never to drink and drive again. However, she has kept the Breathalyzer attached to her car because it is a comfort to her family. She told everyone, "I'll leave it on my car until I die." **Do you want me to explain that again?**

Step 1 & 2:
1. Listen to your partners read the first parts of the article. If you don't understand something, ask them to explain in different words.
2. Answer their comprehension questions.

Step 3:
1. Read your article to your partners. If they don't understand something, explain with different words.
2. Ask your partners these comprehension questions.

Comprehension Questions

1. What part of the car is the Breathalyzer connected to:
1. Why did she have poor judgment?
2. What happened on the way home from the Chinese restaurant?
3. What happened to her head?
4. What did she promise? Why?
5. Does she still have the Breathalyzer attached to her car? Why?

Step 4: Do the exercise on page 133.

Fluency Writing 6

DO NOT look at the article again. You can ask your partners to give you some details again if you want.

Students

A, B, & C

Step 4: Fluency Writing Exercise

1. Write a paragraph with as many details as you can about "Stopping a Drunk Driver."
    You can use the "Key Words and Phrases" to write your paper.
2. Write about the information from **all three parts of the article** (Part 1, Part 2 and Part 3),
    not just your part.

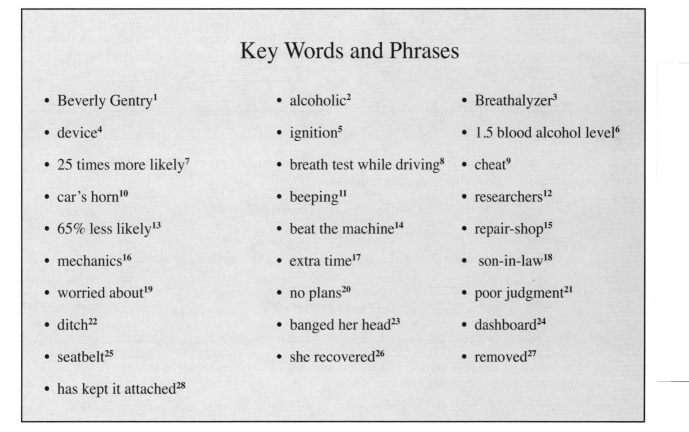

Key Words and Phrases

- Beverly Gentry[1]
- device[4]
- 25 times more likely[7]
- car's horn[10]
- 65% less likely[13]
- mechanics[16]
- worried about[19]
- ditch[22]
- seatbelt[25]
- has kept it attached[28]

- alcoholic[2]
- ignition[5]
- breath test while driving[8]
- beeping[11]
- beat the machine[14]
- extra time[17]
- no plans[20]
- banged her head[23]
- she recovered[26]

- Breathalyzer[3]
- 1.5 blood alcohol level[6]
- cheat[9]
- researchers[12]
- repair-shop[15]
- son-in-law[18]
- poor judgment[21]
- dashboard[24]
- removed[27]

A

Student

Fluency Writing 7

DO NOT LOOK AT YOUR PARTNERS' PAGES.

Before Step 1:

1. Silently read the article below.
2. Write answers to the comprehension questions below.

Sleep for Students (part 1)

Many high schools start at 7:30 a.m., which sleep experts say is too early for the students. For teenagers, sleepiness in the early morning is a result of human biology. ***Do you understand?*** For all humans, sleepiness is caused by a certain hormone, in other words, a type of chemical in our bodies. In young children and adults, our bodies produce this "sleep" hormone at around 8 or 9 p.m. , so we begin to feel sleepy at that time. ***OK?*** In contrast, teenagers' bodies produce the hormone later in the evening, at around 11 p.m., and it remains in their bodies until about 8 a.m. As a result, even if teenagers try to get more sleep by going to bed earlier, they will probably still be sleepy until 8 a.m. This problem with sleep is causing students to feel moody; in other words, they may be angry for no good reason, or they may feel depressed. ***Understand?***

Because of this discovery about teenagers' sleep patterns, some high schools are trying to start later in the morning. In one city, they changed the starting time from 7:30 to 8:45. ***Got it?***

Step 1:

1. Read your article to your partner. If they don't understand something, explain with different words.
2. Ask your partner these comprehension questions.

Comprehension Questions

1. How do many teenagers feel at 7:30 a.m.?

2. At what time is the sleep hormone produced in young children and adults?

   At what time for teenagers?

3. Why doesn't it help teenagers to go to bed earlier?

Step 2:

1. Listen to your partner read the second part of the article. If you don't understand something, ask them to explain in different words.
2. Answer their comprehension questions.

Step 3: Do the exercise on page 136.

Fluency Writing 7

DO NOT LOOK AT YOUR PARTNERS' PAGES.

Before Step 1
1. Silently read the article below.
2. Write answers to the comprehension questions below.

Sleep for Students (part 2)

This is the second part of the article.

In the first part, it said that some schools are trying to start later in the morning. The results of this change have been remarkable. Students report that they are feeling less depressed. Their grades are improving. Parents say that their teenage children are less moody. Teachers report that students are tardy and absent less often. *Do you understand the word "tardy"?*

However, there are people who think that starting high school later is not a good idea. They have two main criticisms. First, many students and teacher complain that a later start means a later end to the school day. This pushes athletic practice and other after-school activities into the dark hours of the evening. Other students complain that the new schedule interferes with their part-time jobs. *Got it?*

A second criticism of the new schedule is that starting class so late does not prepare teenagers for the future. Traditionally, most full-time jobs start at 8 p.m., so some people feel that it is important for teenagers to establish the pattern of waking up early. This habit will help teenagers when they graduate from school and begin working full-time. *Do you want me to repeat that?*

Step 1:
1. Listen to your partner read the first part of the article. If you don't understand something, ask them to explain in different words.
2. Answer their comprehension questions.

Step 2:
1. Read your article to your partner. If they don't understand something, explain with different words.
2. Ask your partner these comprehension questions.

Comprehension Questions
1. Some high schools are starting later:
   • How do students feel as a result of this change?
   • How are students' grades?
   • What do parents say?
   • What do teachers say?
2. The first criticism is that the school day ends later. Why is that an inconvenience?
3. Explain the second criticism of the new schedule.

Step 3: Do the exercise on page 136.

Fluency Writing 7

Students
A & B

Step 4: Fluency Writing Exercise

1. Write a paragraph with as many details as you can about "Sleep for Students."
   You can use the "Key Words and Phrases" to write your paper.
2. Write about the information from **both parts of the article** (Part 1 and Part 2),
   not just your part.

Key Words and Phrases

- 7:30 a.m.[1]
- sleep experts[2]
- teenagers[3]
- human biology[4]
- hormone[5]
- young children and adults[6]
- 11 p.m.[7]
- 8 a.m.[8]
- moody[9]
- for no good reason[10]
- depressed[11]
- start later[12]
- 8:45 a.m.[13]
- remarkable[14]
- grades[15]
- tardy/absent[16]
- criticism[17]
- later start / later end[18]
- athletic practice/activities[19]
- interfere with[20]
- part-time jobs[21]
- full-time jobs[22]
- establish pattern of[23]
- habit will help[24]

Fluency Writing 8

DO NOT LOOK AT YOUR PARTNERS' PAGES.

Before Step 1:
1. Silently read the article below.
2. Write answers to the comprehension questions below.

Unattractive Men (part 1)

Researchers wanted to compare two groups of men. When the first group of men were in high school, they were considered attractive. In contrast, when the second group of men were in high school, they were not considered very attractive. The researchers were interested in learning whether there was an advantage in later life for the good-looking men. *Understand?*

This research began in 1955. Research assistants looked at the boys' pictures in a high school year book and gave a score to each boy for their appearance. *Do you understand what a "year book" is?* Then, 40 years later, they contacted these boys, who were now men between 50 and 60 years old, and asked them questions about their life. *OK?*

Here are some of the results. First, the least attractive men had the most education. They also had received the best grades in school.

Concerning job status, the unattractive men had the higher status. *Do you understand what "job status" means?* In fact, the higher the score which a man got on attractiveness, the lower his job status was in later life. *Got it?*

Step 1:
1. Read your article to your partner. If they don't understand something, explain with different words.
2. Ask your partner these comprehension questions.

Comprehension Questions
1. Which two groups did researchers compare?
2. What was the purpose of the research?
3. How did the research assistants use the high school year books?
4. How old are the men now?
5. What did the researchers find out about education? Also, how about grades?
6. What did they learn about job status?

Step 2:
1. Listen to your partner read the second part of the article. If you don't understand something, ask them to explain in different words.
2. Answer their comprehension questions.

Step 3: Do the exercise on page 139.

Fluency Writing 8

DO NOT LOOK AT YOUR PARTNERS' PAGES.

Before Step 1:
1. Silently read the article below.
2. Write answers to the comprehension questions below.

Unattractive Men (part 2)

This is the second part of the article.

As it said in Part 1, researchers compared two groups of boys. The first group of boys were considered attractive in high school, and the second group were not considered very attractive. Now, these two groups of boys are men between the ages of 50 and 60 years old. Researchers asked the men some questions about their life in order to find out if there were any differences between the two groups. One discovery was that the less attractive men had a serious relationship with a female at a later age than the attractive men. *OK?*

Researchers gave a possible explanation for this result. Homely boys (in other words, unattractive ones) might be socially handicapped in high school. *Do you understand what "socially handicapped" means?* In other words, their social life was not very active. Then, because their social life was not very active, they were able to focus on their education. This resulted in a higher job status later in life. *Understand?*

Researchers also found that attractive men tended to have less-educated wives. Perhaps the reason for this is that handsome boys had girlfriends in high school and college, and, as a result, they became less interested in education. Also, they got married at an early age to younger women who probably also had less education. *Got it?*

Step 1:
1. Listen to your partner read the first part of the article. If you don't understand something, ask them to explain in different words.
2. Answer their comprehension questions.

Step 2:
1. Read your article to your partner. If they don't understand something, explain with different words.
2. Ask your partner these comprehension questions.

Comprehension Questions

1. What did the researchers learn about serious relationships with females?

2. Who was perhaps more socially handicapped?

3. What was the result of being socially handicapped?

4. Which group of men had less-educated wives?

5. How do the researchers explain the reason for the less-educated wives?

Step 3: Do the exercise on page 139.

Fluency Writing 8

Students

A & B

Step 4: Fluency Writing Exercise

1. Write a paragraph with as many details as you can about "Unattractive Men." You can use the "Key Words and Phrases" to write your paper.
2. Write about the information from **both parts of the article** (Part 1 and Part 2), not just your part.

Key Words and Phrases

- two groups[1]
- unattractive[3]
- 1955[5]
- year book[7]
- appearance[9]
- 50 to 60 years old[11]
- education[13]
- job status[15]
- discovery[17]
- later age[19]
- homely[21]
- social life[23]
- less-educated wives[25]
- at an early age[27]

- attractive[2]
- advantage[4]
- research assistants[6]
- score[8]
- 40 years later[10]
- least attractive[12]
- grades[14]
- higher score / lower score[16]
- serious relationship with a female[18]
- possible explanation[20]
- socially handicapped[22]
- focus on education[24]
- handsome[26]

Section 3: Grammar

Individual Work: Units 1, 2, 5, 6, 7, 8,
10, 11, 13, 14, 15, 17, 18,
19, 20, 22, 23, 24, 26,
27, 29, 30

Group Work Units 3, 4, 9, 12, 16,
21, 25, 28

Unit 1

Subject Nouns and Verb Phrases

Subjects & Main Verbs

- go __   - dogs __   - Bill ✗   - TV __   - return __

- Tom and Sara __   - was __   - heard __   - students __

Note: The subject of a sentence can be a noun or a pronoun.

Exercise 1:

Choose a word from the box above and fill in the blanks with a subject.

1. __*Bill*__ ate his dinner.

2. Before a hard test, all _____ need to study.

3. Our old _____ is having problems.

4. _____ plan to discuss their research project.

5. Three _____ are barking outside my apartment.

Exercise 2:

Choose a word from the box above and fill in the blanks with a verb. The letter "s" over a word tells you that it is a subject.

1. We^s _____ the news about the accident.

    s
1. We _____ the news about the accident.

    s
2. My decision _____ difficult to make.

    s
3. During the week, I always _____ to work at 8 o'clock and _____ home at 5.

Auxiliary Verbs

• was __	• can't __	• will __	• should have __
• is _X_	• had __	• doesn't __	

Note: Auxiliary verbs are "helping" verbs. They work with the main verb to indicate tense, etc.

Exercise 3:

❶. Underline the main verbs.

❷. Choose a word from the box above and fill in the blank with an auxiliary verb.

1. She __*is*__ <u>going</u> on vacation next week.

2. Unfortuately, I _____ find my drivers license.

3. This sandwich _____ taste very good.

4. After the victory, the team _____ given an award.

5. If you _____ wanted me to help, you _____ called me.

6. Steve and Dan _____ take some medicine if they start to feel sick.

Exercise 4: *Note: "to + verb" is an infinitive. It is not the main verb of the sentence.*

❶. <u>Double</u>-underline the infinitives (*to + <u>verb</u>*), for example, to eat, to give, to sing.

❷. <u>Underline</u> the maain verbs.

1. We <u>decided</u> <u>to mail</u> the package.

2. Jane refused to meet me at the airport.

3. Because Ken couldn't see well, he promised to get his eyes examined.

4. The car seemed to run well, so he bought it.

5. If the repairman comes, you need to explain the problem to him.

Exercise 5:

    ❶. Write **S** above the Subjects.

    ❷. Write **V** above the Verbs.

    ❸. Write **AV** above the Auxiliary Verbs (if there are any).

                     S   AV   V

1. Those beautiful birds will return again next year.

                                  S   V

2. Before a tennis game, the players need to practice.
   (Remember: "to practice" is not the verb of the sentence. It is an infinitive)

3. Tom wears glasses, but his brother doesn't.

4. Jim was unhappy to hear the sad news.

5. During the break, everyone could go outside.

6. The history test was given last week, but Ken didn't come.

7. Ann was happy about the end of the movie.

8. My brother and his boss should arrive soon.

9. I didn't need the Internet to find the answer.

10. You can take this medicine twice a day.

11. In case of an emergency, Tom keeps extra money in his closet.

12. He found a surprise inside the envelope.

Exercise 6:

    ❶. Use the patterns to write sentences on the blank lines below.

        Write **S** above the Subjects.

        Write **V** above the Verbs.

        Write **AV** above the Auxiliary Verbs (if there are any).

                      S   V   V

Example: S-V-V: Tony ate dinner and watched TV.

1. S-V: _____

2. S-AV-V: _____

3. S-S-V: _____

4. S-AV-V-S-AV-V: _____

      _____

Conjunctions

S	V	, CONJ	S	V

(conjunction)

, and
, but
, so
, or

Exercise 1:

❶. Write **S** above the Subjects.
❷. Write **V** above the Verbs.
❸. Write **AV** above the Auxiliary Verbs (if there are any).
❹. Write **CONJ** above the conjunctions.

      S   V   CONJ   S   V
1. My sister went to Hawaii, and my brother went to Alaska.

      S V   CONJ S AV V
2. He needs to pass the test, or   he will fail the course.

3. I love short stories,   but   I hate long novels.

4. It might rain,   so   we should take our umbrellas.

5. You should begin to work now,   or   you won't finish on time.

Exercise 2:

❶. Fill in the blanks with a conjunction (and, but, so, or)
❷. Write **S** above the Subjects.
❸. Write **V** above the Verbs.
❹. Write **AV** above the Auxiliary Verbs (if there are any).
❸. Write **CONJ** above the conjunctions.

1. He did the job well, _____ I gave him an extra tip.

2. You should wear a hat on a cold day, _____ you might catch a cold.

3. Most teenagers like to stay up late, _____ they don't like to get up early.

Exercise 3:

❶.Write a sentence with **and**, a sentence with **but**, a sentence with **so**, and a sentence with **or**.
❷.Write **S** above the Subjects.
❸.Write **V** above the Verbs.
❹.Write **AV** above the Auxiliary Verbs (if there are any).
❺.Write **CONJ** above the conjunctions.

1._____

2._____

3._____

4._____

About Group Work

Units 3, 4, 9, 12, 16, 21, 25, and 28 have been
designed for Group Work. In group work, you will
have a page marked "Student A, B, or C."
On your page, you will find a worksheet
and directions explaining what to do with it.

This is very important:

DO NOT LOOK AT YOUR PARTNERS' PAGES.

Unit 3

Subjects, Verbs, Auxiliary Verbs, and Conjunctions

Directions

Read these directions and questions about the worksheet below to your partners.

1. In Sentence A , write **S** and **V** and **AV** above the subjects, verbs and auxiliary verbs.
4. In Sentence C , write **S** and **V** and **AV** above the subjects, verbs and auxiliary verbs.
7. In Sentence D , write **S** and **V** and **AV** above the subjects, verbs and auxiliary verbs.
10. In Sentence E , write **S** and **V** and **AV** above the subjects, verbs and auxiliary verbs.
13. In Sentence F , write **S** and **V** and **AV** above the subjects, verbs and auxiliary verbs.
16. In Sentence G , what is the conjunction?
19. In Sentence H , is there a problem with the verbs?
22. In Sentence J, what do we call the grammar mistake in this sentence? Write the name of the mistake in the blank.

Worksheet

A. My father doesn't know how to use e-mail, so he always writes me letters.

B. I woke early today and finished my homework.

C. Tom cooks the meals, his roommate washes dishes. (_____)

D. My friends secretly planned a party for me, so I was surprised.

E. Ann complained about the food, Sue liked it.

F. It began to rain we went into the house. (_____)

G. The traffic was heavy on our way home so we decided to take a short cut.

H. Last night, we looked at the sky, and we see many stars.

I. At the zoo, the animals were in their cages, they looked hungry. (_____)

J. His car ran out of gas he decided to walk to the gas station. (_____)

Directions

Read these directions and questions about the worksheet below to your partners.

2. In Sentence B, write **S** and **V** and **AV** above the subjects, verbs, and auxiliary verbs.

5. There is a grammar mistake in Sentence C. It is called a "comma splice." The problem is that there are two sentences joined together with a comma, but there is no conjunction. In the blank write "comma splice."

8. In Sentence D, is "can't" a verb or auxiliary verb?

11. In Sentence E, is this a comma splice? Explain.

14. There is a grammar mistake in Sentence F. It is called a "run on." The problem is that there are two sentences joined together, but there is no conjunction or a period between them. In the blank write "run on."

17. In Sentence G, put a comma in this sentence.

20. In Sentence I, what do we call the grammar mistake in this sentence? Write the name of the mistake in the blank.

23. In Sentence J, how can we correct the mistake in this sentence?

Worksheet

A. My father doesn't know how to use e-mail, so he always writes me letters.

B. I woke early today and finished my homework.

C. Tom cooks the meals, his roommate washes dishes. (_____)

D. My friends secretly planned a party for me, so I was surprised..

E. Ann complained about the food, Sue liked it.

F. It began to rain we went into the house. (_____)

G. The traffic was heavy on our way home so we decided to take a short cut.

H. Last night, we looked at the sky, and we see many stars.

I. At the zoo, the animals were in their cages, they looked hungry. (_____)

J. His car ran out of gas he decided to walk to the gas station. (_____)

Directions

Read these directions and questions about the worksheet below to your partners.

3. In Sentence B, is it necessary to put a subject after the word "and?"

6. In Sentence C, put a conjunction after the comma or change the comma to a period.

9. In Sentence D, is this sentence a comma splice? Why or why not?

12. In Sentence E, how can we correct the problem?

15. In Sentence F, put a conjunction or put in a period between the two sentences.

18. In Sentence H, write **S** and **V** and **AV** above the subjects, verbs and the auxiliary verbs

21. In Sentence I, how can we correct the grammar problem in this sentence?

24. In Sentence J, circle the infinitive in this sentence.

Worksheet

A. My father doesn't know how to use e-mail, so he always writes me letters.

B. I woke early today and finished my homework.

C. Tom cooks the meals, his roommate washes dishes. (_____)

D. My friends secretly planned a party for me, so I was surprised.

E. Ann complained about the food, Sue liked it.

F. It began to rain we went into the house. (_____)

G. The traffic was heavy on our way home so we decided to take a short cut.

H. Last night, we looked at the sky, and we see many stars.

I. At the zoo, the animals were in their cages, they looked hungry. (_____)

J. His car ran out of gas he decided to walk to the gas station. (_____)

Grammar Unit 3: *Subjects, Verbs, Auxiliary Verbs, and Conjunctions* • 149

Unit 4

Prepositions

Directions

Read these directions and questions about the worksheet below to your partners.
1. Look at A. There is a square. Above it is a dot. In the blank finish the word "above.""Above" is a preposition.
4. Look at D. Draw a dot next to the square. Write the word "next to".
7. Look at E. In Sentence F, fill in the blanks with the appropriate prepositions.
10. Look at I. Circle the 15 prepositions.
13. In Sentence J, above the word "bed," write the word "noun."
16. In Sentence L, circle the prepositions and underline the prepositional phrases.
19. In Sentence N, underline the three prepositional phrases.

Preposition Worksheet

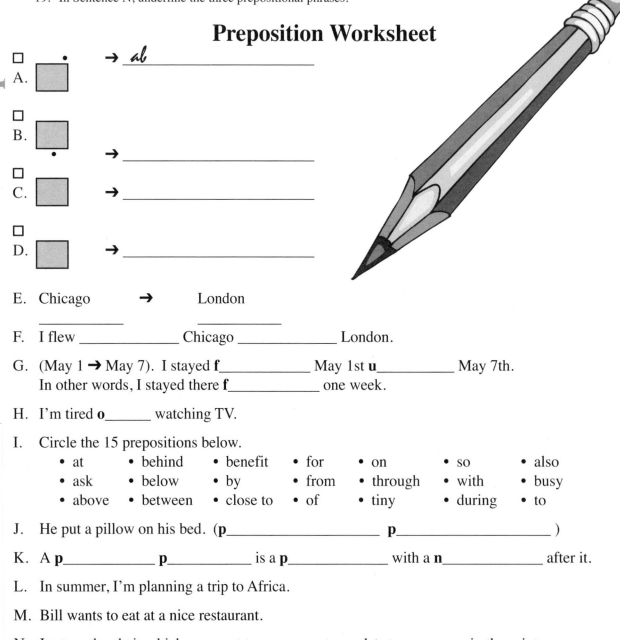

A. → *ab*_____

B.

C. → _____

D. → _____

E. Chicago → London

_____   _____

F. I flew _____ Chicago _____ London.

G. (May 1 → May 7). I stayed **f**_____ May 1st **u**_____ May 7th.
In other words, I stayed there **f**_____ one week.

H. I'm tired **o**_____ watching TV.

I. Circle the 15 prepositions below.
- at
- behind
- benefit
- for
- on
- so
- also
- ask
- below
- by
- from
- through
- with
- busy
- above
- between
- close to
- of
- tiny
- during
- to

J. He put a pillow on his bed. (**p**_____ **p**_____)

K. A **p**_____ **p**_____ is a **p**_____ with a **n**_____ after it.

L. In summer, I'm planning a trip to Africa.

M. Bill wants to eat at a nice restaurant.

N. I sat on the chair which was next to my computer and put some paper in the printer.

Directions

Read these directions and questions about the worksheet below to your partners.

2. Look at B. What preposition describes the position of the dot? Write it in the blank.
5. Look at E. Under the name "Chicago," write the word "from."
8. Look at G. Fill in the blanks with prepositions.
11. In Sentence J, circle the preposition.
14. In Sentence J, the phrase "on his bed" is a prepositional phrase.
    In the blanks, write the expression "prepositional phrase."
17. In Sentence M, is the word "to" a preposition or part of an infinitive?

Preposition Worksheet

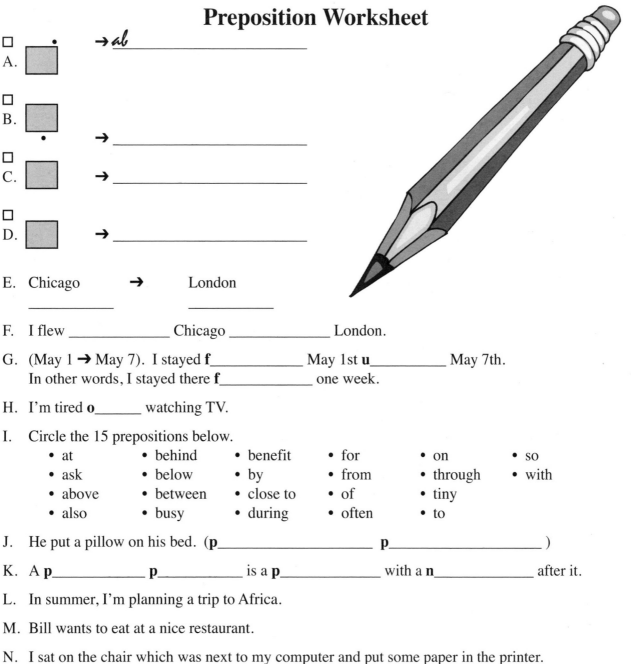

A. □ ▢ · → *ab*_____

B. □ ▢

C. □ ▢ · → _____

D. □ ▢ → _____

E. Chicago → London
   _____   _____

F. I flew _____ Chicago _____ London.

G. (May 1 → May 7). I stayed **f**_____ May 1st **u**_____ May 7th.
   In other words, I stayed there **f**_____ one week.

H. I'm tired **o**_____ watching TV.

I. Circle the 15 prepositions below.
   - at   - behind   - benefit   - for   - on   - so
   - ask   - below   - by   - from   - through   - with
   - above   - between   - close to   - of   - tiny
   - also   - busy   - during   - often   - to

J. He put a pillow on his bed. (**p**_____ **p**_____)

K. A **p**_____ **p**_____ is a **p**_____ with a **n**_____ after it.

L. In summer, I'm planning a trip to Africa.

M. Bill wants to eat at a nice restaurant.

N. I sat on the chair which was next to my computer and put some paper in the printer.

C

Directions

Read these directions and questions about the worksheet below to your partners.

3. Look at C. Draw a dot inside the square. Fill in the blanks with the words "in" and "inside."
    These words are prepositions.

6. Look at E. Write the word "to" under "London."

9. In Sentence H, fill in the blank with a preposition.

12. In Sentence J, underline the words "on his bed."

15. In Sentence K, fill in the blanks with these words: "A prepositional phrase is a preposition with a noun phrase
    after it." (A noun phrase can have an article (a, the) or an adjective before the noun.)

18. In Sentence M, what is the prepositional phrase? Underline it.

Preposition Worksheet

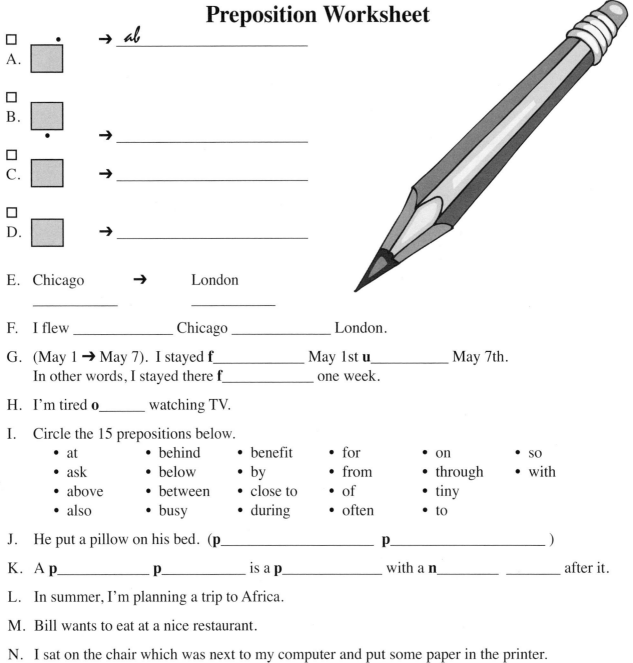

A. ☐ → *ab*_____

B. ☐

C. ☐ → _____

D. ☐ → _____

E. Chicago ➡ London
    _____   _____

F. I flew _____ Chicago _____ London.

G. (May 1 ➡ May 7). I stayed **f**_____ May 1st **u**_____ May 7th.
    In other words, I stayed there **f**_____ one week.

H. I'm tired **o**_____ watching TV.

I. Circle the 15 prepositions below.
    - at   - behind   - benefit   - for   - on   - so
    - ask   - below   - by   - from   - through   - with
    - above   - between   - close to   - of   - tiny
    - also   - busy   - during   - often   - to

J. He put a pillow on his bed. (**p**_____ **p**_____)

K. A **p**_____ **p**_____ is a **p**_____ with a **n**_____ _____ after it.

L. In summer, I'm planning a trip to Africa.

M. Bill wants to eat at a nice restaurant.

N. I sat on the chair which was next to my computer and put some paper in the printer.

Unit 5

Prepositions, Prepositional Phrases, and Gerunds

Exercise 1:

Underline the preposition(s) in each sentence.

1. They built their new home on a hill.
2. The reason for my absence is that the bus was late.
3. I wrote a letter to Sue from Seattle. (two prepositions)
4. Tom wanted to put his piano by the window.
   (***Notice:*** "to" *in this sentence is not a preposition; it is part of the infinitive.*)

Exercise 2:

❶. Double underline the preposition(s) in each sentence.
❷. Underline the prepositional phrases in each sentence.
   (prepositional phrase = the preposition and the noun that follows it)

1. She bought a new CD at the store.
2. As soon as I walked through the door, I knew something was wrong.
3. Allen came to my house with a book that was for my sister.
4. I'm planning to move to a new apartment in autumn.

Exercise 3:

❶. Double underline the preposition(s) in each sentence.
❷. Write the gerund form of the verb after it.
   [gerund = verb-ing that acts like a noun. (pulling / sleeping / watching)]

1. I gained some weight from *eating* (eat) too much ice cream.
2. My roommate and I talked about _____ (move) soon.
3. This computer should not be used for _____ (send) e-mail.
4. My boss talked to us about _____ (work) past midnight.
5. Information about _____ (buy) cheap tickets and _____ (make) reservations is helpful for travelers.

Exercise 4:

❶. Circle the preposition(s) in each sentence.
❷. Complete the sentences with a gerund (verb-ing).

1. My brother is good at _____
2. Ann became sick from _____
3. I'm tired of _____
4. Tom is interested in _____

Unit 6

Phrases,
Dependent and Independent Clauses

(Clause = a group of words that include a subject and verb)

Exercise 1:

❶. Write **S** / **V** / **AV** above the Subjects / Verbs / Auxiliary Verbs.

❷. If there is an **S** and **V**, write **clause** in the blank.

❸. If there is **no S** and **V**, write **phrase** in the blank.

                                          S   V

clause   1. they climbed the mountain

phrase   2. for a lot of money

_____   3. while I was sleeping

_____   4. during the night

_____   5. Tom was trying to avoid his boss

_____   6. because the city had no money

_____   7. in an emergency

_____   8. by midnight

_____   9. by the time she arrived

An **independent clause** can be a sentence.

A **dependent clause** cannot be a sentence.

Exercise 2:

❶. In the blanks, write **I** (independent) if the words can be a sentence.

❷. In the blanks, write **D** (dependent) if the words cannot be a sentence.

I 1. the rich man gave some money to the charity

D 2. after the airport was closed

___ 3. which happened in summer

___ 4. they failed to complete the work on time

___ 5. the customers became upset

___ 6. when the patient recovered from his illness

___ 7. Sue gave a good explanation

___ 8. whom I will take to the dance

Exercise 3:

❶. Underline the dependent clauses.

❷. Write **S / V / AV** above the Subjects / Verbs / Auxiliary Verbs in the independent clauses.

❸. Write **s / v / av** above the subjects / verbs / auxiliary verbs in the dependent clauses.

      S   AV   V   s   v

1. He didn't want to go <u>because it seemed dangerous.</u>

            S   s   v   V

2. The parents <u>who attended the meeting</u> learned about the club.

3. After we had discussed the plans, we decided to start over.

4. We can make more money if we work harder now.

5. The nurse whom I like the best is always cheerful.

6. While Ken was writing the report, the phone rang.

Common Mistakes

- Putting two independent clauses together:

        S   V   ,   S   V
      Peter gave a speech, the audience listened. *(CS = comma splice)*

        S   V   S   AV   V
      The room was a mess he couldn't find his keys. *(RO = run on)*

- Using a dependent clause and no independent clause:
      Because Jim's birthday is tomorrow. *(frag = fragment)*

Exercise 4:

Correct the mistakes explained in the box above.

1. *(Mistake)* Peter gave a speech, the audience listened.

   Peter gave a speech _____

3. *(Mistake)* The room was a mess he couldn't find his keys.

   The room was a mess _____

5. *(Mistake)* Because Jim's birthday is tomorrow.

   Because Jim's birthday is tomorrow, _____

Exercise 5:

❶. Write **OK** if the sentence is grammatically correct.
❷. Write **CS** if it is a comma splice, **RO** if it is a run on, and **frag** if it is a fragment.
❸. If the sentences have a mistake, write them again correctly.

_____*CS*_____ 1. I trained my dog, now he can do some tricks.

*I trained my dog. Now, he can do some tricks.*

_____ 2. Although John read the book carefully.

_____

_____ 3. The clock stopped, so I was late for my appointment.

_____

_____ 4. The clerk at the store gave Sally a plastic bag it broke on her way home.

_____

_____ 5. Because we couldn't get tickets to the concert.

_____

_____ 6. Our hotel room had a fireplace, it made us feel relaxed.

_____

_____ 7. Don arrived late at the ticket counter there were no tickets left.

_____

Exercise 6:

❶ Use the words in the box to write four sentences with dependent and independent clauses.
❷. Underline the dependent clauses.
❸. Write **S / V / AV** above the Subjects / Verbs / Auxiliary Verbs in the **independent clauses**.
❹. Write **s / v / av** above the subjects / verbs / auxiliary verbs in the **dependent clauses**.

• before • when • because • if

_____

_____

_____

_____

Unit 7
Wish and *Hope*

Exercise 1:

❶. Write **Right** next to the correct sentences.
❷. Write **Wrong** next to the incorrect ones.

Right ____ 1. I wish that it would rain.

Wrong ____ 2. I hope that it would rain.

_____ 3. I hope that it will rain.

_____ 4. I wish that he will call me.

_____ 5. I wish that he would call me.

_____ 6. I hope that he will call me.

_____ 7. They wish the game will be cancelled.

_____ 8. They hope the game will be cancelled.

_____ 9. He wishes that he didn't have to work tonight.

_____10. He hopes that he will not have to work tonight.

Exercise 2: Write **hope** or **wish** in the blanks of the rule below.

> ### *Rule*
> • _____ + past tense or "would"
> • _____ + future tense

Exercise 3: Complete the sentences with a subject + wish or hope.

1. _____ my father would give me a new car.

2. _____ my sister had her own room.

3. _____ next winter will not be too cold.

4. _____ you will finish your homework.

5. _____ I lived in the countryside.

6. _____ I will live in the countryside.

7. _____ his friend will get a good job after graduating.

Unit 8

Relative *Who* Clauses

Exercise 1:

❶. Read the sentences.
❷. Answer the questions about the sentences.

Sentence A: The woman comes from Germany.

Question 1: Do we know which woman comes from Germany?

Sentence B: The woman who gives piano lessons at my school comes from Germany.

Question 2: Now do we know which woman comes from Germany?

Sentence C: Don Wilson is my best friend.

Question 3: Do we know who my best friend is?

Sentence D: Don Wilson, who is a terrible golfer, is my best friend.

Question 4: Do we need the information "who is a terrible golfer" to know who my best friend is?

Question 5: Are there commas in Sentence D?

Sentence E: The man is happy.

Question 6: Do we know which man is happy?

Question 7: Do we need more information in order to know which man is happy?

Sentence F: The man who won the prize is happy.

Question 8: Now do we know which man is happy?

Question 9: Do we need the clause "who won the prize" in order to know which man was happy?

Question 10: Are there commas in Sentence F?

Sentence G: My father sold a painting for $500.

Question 11: Do we know who sold a painting?

Question 12: Do we need more information to know who sold a painting?

Sentence H: My father, who is very talented, sold one of his paintings for $500.

Question 13: Do we need the clause "who is very talented" in order to know who sold the painting?

Question 14: Are there commas in Sentence H?

Exercise 2:

❶. Read the sample sentences.

❷. Look at the Rules in the box below and choose a or b.

Sample sentence 1:
   Michael Jordan, who was a famous basketball player, likes to buy flowers for his wife.
Sample sentence 2:
   The man who lives next door to me likes to buy flowers for his wife.

Rule 1: We put commas around the relative "who" clause if the information is _____
   (choose)
   a. needed in order to know who the person is.
   b. extra information about the person.

Rule 2: We do not put commas around the relative "who" clause if the information is _____
   (choose)
   a. needed in order to know who the person is.
   b. extra information about the person.

Exercise 3:

❶. Underline the relative "who" clause.

❷. In the blank, write **Needed** if we need the information to know who the person is. . .

❸. In the blank, write **Extra** if we do not need the information to know who the person is. . .

extra _____ 1. Sam Thompson, <u>who is the owner of our company</u>, has a yacht.

_____ 2. Our classmate who has a tattoo of a monkey on his arm will tell us why getting a tattoo is not a good idea.

_____ 3. Steve, who always complains about the weather, is moving to Hawaii.

_____ 4. At the computer store, the salesman who sold me a printer was very knowledgeable.

Exercise 4:

❶. Write **Needed** or **Extra** in the blanks.

❷. Put in commas if the relative "who" clause is extra. You need to put in five commas.

_____ 1. I have a roommate. My roommate who is a waiter often makes a lot of money from tips.

_____ 2. I have three roommates. The roommate who can speak four languages always helps me with my homework.

_____ 3. The boy who was caught shoplifting is at the police station.

_____ 4. When I was a child, I always spent my afternoons with my grandfather who was my mother's father.

_____ 5. Because she hurt her elbow, Jane has an appointment with Dr. Olsen who is a great doctor.

_____ 6. During the flight, Susan talked to the stewardess, Ann Brooks. Ann who has traveled all over the world told Susan about some of her adventures.

Unit 9

Verb Tenses

Directions

Read these directions and questions about the worksheet below to your partners.
Note: Perfect and continuous verbs include an auxiliary verb.

1. Look at Sentence A. Is the verb in the present or past tense?
4. Look at Sentence C. Should we fill in the blank with "leave" or "left?" Why?
7. Look at Sentence E. Write the letters "PC" above the auxiliary verb and main verb that is past continuous and write the word "past" above the verb that is past tense.
10. Look at Sentence F. Why don't we use the past continuous tense with the second verb "stop?"
13. Look at Sentence I. Circle the word "after." Then underline the verbs.
16. Look at Sentence J. Underline the auxiliary verbs and verbs. Then circle the word "before."
19. Look at Sentence L. Circle the correct answers.
22. Look at Sentence O. Should one of these verbs be past perfect? Why or why not?

Worksheet

A. They worked hard.

B. It is time to begin.

C. When they arrived, I _____ the house.

D. *Past continuous verb tense shows that an action* _____
   _____

E. My father fell asleep while he was watching the movie.

F. While she was using the computer, the electricity stopped.

G. Ken _____ *(to turn on)* the radio while he _____ *(to drive)* to
   work yesterday.

H. *Past perfect verb tense shows that something* _____
   _____

I. After he had already learned some Spanish, he visited Mexico.

J. The pilot had told the passengers to fasten their seatbelts before he started to land.

K. **Past perfect:** Usually, in sentences with past perfect verb tense, we have (one/more than one) verb.

L. **Past perfect:** We use past perfect verb tense with the action that happened (first/second).
   The action that happened (first/second) is past tense.

M. He _____ *(to write)* a letter to the actor after he _____ *(to see)* the movie.

N. They took a trip to Bali.

O. While he was cooking dinner, the phone rang.

Directions

Read these directions and questions about the worksheet below to your partners.
Note: Perfect and continuous verbs include an auxiliary verb.

  2. Look at Sentence B. Change the verb to past tense.
  5. Look at Sentence D. I'm going to dictate a grammar rule to you. Please write this in the blank: Past continuous verb tense shows that an action was happening. It is often used with the word "while."
  8. Look at Sentence F. Underline the auxiliary verbs and main verbs.
  1. Look at Sentence G. Write the correct form of the two verbs.
14. Look at Sentence I. Write the word "past" above the verb that is past. Write the letters "PP" above the auxiliary verb and main verb that is past perfect.
17. Look at Sentence J. Which action happened first?
20. Look at Sentence M. Write the verbs in the correct form.

Worksheet

A. They worked hard.

B. It is time to begin.

C. When they arrived, I _____ the house.

D. *Past continuous verb tense shows that an action* _____
   _____

E. My father fell asleep while he was watching the movie.

F. While she was using the computer, the electricity stopped.

G. Ken _____ *(to turn on)* the radio while he _____ *(to drive)* to
   work yesterday.

H. *Past perfect verb tense shows that something* _____
   _____

 I. After he had already learned some Spanish, he visited Mexico.

 J. The pilot had told the passengers to fasten their seatbelts before he started to land.

K. **Past perfect:** Usually, in sentences with past perfect verb tense, we have (one/more than one) verb.

L. **Past perfect:** We use past perfect verb tense with the action that happened (first/second).
   The action that happened (first/second) is past tense.

M. He _____ *(to write)* a letter to the actor after he _____ *(to see)* the movie.

N. They took a trip to Bali.

O. While he was cooking dinner, the phone rang.

Directions

Read these directions and questions about the worksheet below to your partners.
Note: Perfect and continuous verbs include an auxiliary verb.

3. Look at Sentence C. What is the verb of the dependent clause?
6. Look at Sentence E. Underline the auxiliary verbs and main verbs.
9. Look at Sentence F. Write the letters "PC" above the auxiliary verb and verb that is past continuous and write the word "past" above the verb that is past tense.
12. Look at Sentence H. I'm going to dictate a grammar rule to you. Please write this in the blank: Past Perfect verb tense shows that something happened before another action. It is often used with the words "before," "after," and "already."
15. Look at Sentence I. Which action happened first: visited Mexico or learned Spanish?
18. Look at Sentence K. Circle the correct answer.
21. Look at Sentence N. What is the verb? Should it be past perfect? Why or why not?

Worksheet

A. They worked hard.

B. It is time to begin.

C. When they arrived, I _____ the house.

D. *Past continuous verb tense shows that an action* _____

    _____

E. My father fell asleep while he was watching the movie.

F. While she was using the computer, the electricity stopped.

G. Ken _____ *(to turn on)* the radio while he _____ *(to drive)* to

    work yesterday.

H. *Past perfect verb tense shows that something* _____

    _____

I. After he had already learned some Spanish, he visited Mexico.

J. The pilot had told the passengers to fasten their seatbelts before he started to land.

K. **Past perfect:** Usually, in sentences with past perfect verb tense, we have (one/more than one) verb.

L. **Past perfect:** We use past perfect verb tense with the action that happened (first/second).

    The action that happened (first/second) is past tense.

M. He _____ *(to write)* a letter to the actor after he _____ *(to see)* the movie.

N. They took a trip to Bali.

O. While he was cooking dinner, the phone rang.

Unit 10
Verb Tenses

Exercise 1: Fill in the blanks with the correct words from the box.

• was reading __	• started __	• had finished __	• was studying __
• had practiced __	• went ✗	• played __	• ran __
• was eating __	• watched __	• finished __	

Simple Past
1. She __*went*__ home.
2. Dan _____ his homework early.
3. When the rain _____, we _____ inside the house. *(Two actions happen at the same time.)*

Past Continuous (It shows an action was happening.)
4. Sara _____ the newspaper when her brother arrived.
5. He _____ dinner, while Ann _____ her math.

Past Perfect (It shows an action happened before a second action. Often it is used with "before," "after," *and* "already.") There must be two verbs in the sentence.

6. After he _____ his homework, he _____ TV.
7. The children _____ throwing a ball before they _____ the game.

Three Rules for using Past Perfect

- There are two actions in a sentence. Both happened in the past.
- The action that happened first uses **had + past participle**.
- The action that happened second uses **simple past tense**.

Exercise 2: Read the sentences and answer the questions.

Sentence A. After he had found his new job, he bought a house.

Question 1: Which action happened first? _____

Question 2: What is the verb tense of the action that happened first: simple past or past perfect? ___

Sentence B: When Tom's daughter got home, he had already made dinner for her.

Question 3: Which action happened first? _____

Question 4: What is the verb tense of the action that happened first: simple past or past perfect? ___

Exercise 3:

❶. Underline the auxiliary verbs and main verbs.
❷. Write the verb tenses.

past continuous / simple past 1. She <u>was sleeping</u> when the storm <u>started</u>.

_____ 2. I washed the car.

_____ 3. Tom took a shower, after he had done his exercises,.

_____ 4. They had put new tires on the car before they sold it.

_____ 5. As he was waiting for his ride, he saw an accident.

Exercise 4:

Complete the sentences with simple past, past continuous, or past perfect verb tense.

1. After my dog had run out of the house, _____

2. When _____, he called the fire department.

3. Last night, _____

4. While _____

5. Before _____

Exercise 5:

❶. Underline all the helping verbs and verbs.
❷. If they are the wrong verb tense, write the correct form above them.
(There are a total of ten mistakes.)

started

The first day of last winter vacation was an especially happy time for Ted. It <u>starts</u> on December

20th. He had finished his last test before he had driven back to his hometown. When he arrived at

home, his mother prepares dinner. He was happy to be home. First, he had called his friends to make

plans. Then he unpacked his suitcase. After he does that, he borrowed his father's car and drives into

town. In town, many people are shopping. Ted also needed to do some shopping. While he was

looking at a watch to buy his father, he sees a ring that he wants to give his mother. He doesn't have

enough money with him, so he had to go to the bank.

Unit 11
Reported Speech

Exercise 1: Fill in the blanks with the correct words from the boxes.

| • they __ • she __ • he _X_ • would __ • wanted __ • were __ • the next day __ |

1. *(Direct speech)* Steve said, "**I want** a new job."

   (Reported speech) Steve said that _he_ _____ a new job.

2. *(Direct)* Jane said, "**They are** going to need some help."

   (Reported) Jane said that _____ _____ going to need some help.

3. *(Direct)* Sarah said, "**I will** buy a train ticket **tomorrow**."

   (Reported) Sarah said that _____ _____ buy a train ticket _____

| • had __ • could __ • should __ • our __ • he __ • we __ |

4. *(Direct)* Gordon said, "I **walked** to work **today**."

   (Reported) Gordon said that _____ _____ walked to work today.

5. *(Direct)* Ron said to us, "**You can** start your work **now**."

   (Reported) Ron said that _____ _____ start _____ work now.

6. *(Direct)* Tina said, "Don **should** talk about his experiences."

   (Reported) Tina said that Don _____ talk about his experiences.

| • that __ • had __ • if __ • if __ • was __ • I __ • could __ • she __ • worked __ |

7. *(Direct)* He asked, "Who is this girl?"

   (Reported) He asked who _____ girl _____

8. *(Direct)* Jim asked me, "Where do you work?"

   (Reported) Jim asked where _____

9. *(Direct)* Fred asked, "Does she have a passport?"

   (Reported) Fred asked _____ _____ _____ a passport.

10. *(Direct)* Sue asked Tony, "Can you help me tonight?"

    (Reported) Sue asked Tony _____ he _____ help her tonight.

| • had __ | • to __ | • was __ | • us __ | • turn __ | • told __ | • told __ |

11. *(Direct)* Ken said to Jill and me, "A storm **is** coming."

  (Reported) Ken _____ _____ that a storm _____ coming.

12. *(Direct)* My mother **said** to me, "**Turn off** the lights."

  (Reported) My mother _____ me _____ _____ off the lights.

Exercise 2: Change these quotations (direct speech) to reported speech.

1. Ann said, "I have to do a book report tomorrow."

  (Reported) _____

2. The clerk said to me, "You will need more stamps for your letter."

  (Reported) _____

3. Betty asked, "Where does he live?"

  (Reported) _____

4. The man said, "I should go on a diet."

  (Reported) _____

5. The foreigner said to me, "You are speaking too fast."

  (Reported) _____

6. Jim asked, "Who will they invite to the party tonight?"

  (Reported) _____

7. His boss said to them, "Finish this work before you go home today."

  (Reported) _____

8. Ken asked me, "Do you like pizza?"

  (Reported) _____

Exercise 3:

  ❶. On a separate sheet, write 3 sentences in **Direct Speech**. One of the sentences should be a question.

  ❷. Write the same same sentences in **Reported Speech**.

Exercise 4:

Correct all the reported speech mistakes.

I read this amazing true story in the newspaper. One day, a woman named Barbara was shopping. As she was putting her groceries in her car, a man named Frank walked up to her and showed her his gun. He said get in your car. *told her to get in her car* She said just take my car. He forced her to get into the car with him. They drove to a cash machine and he said put your card in the machine and take out $1000. She said that I can't because I forgot my identification. Next, they drove to a big department store. Frank told Barbara that he wants her to write a check for $6000. After writing the check, Barbara told him that she has to go to the bathroom. In the bathroom, she saw another woman and asked her can you help me. The woman was too frightened and left. Frank forced Barbara to drive to a fast food restaurant and made her pay for $40 worth of hamburgers. She asked him who is he buying all this food for. Afterwards, they went to another store and bought computers, VCRs, and other electronics. He also told her buy 40 cartons of cigarettes. After they left, the store manager called the police and told them I think there is something strange about that couple. The police caught Frank. Barbara said that she is relieved.

Unit 12

Conjunctive Adverbs

Directions

Read these directions and questions about the worksheet below to your partners.

1. Look at Sentences A-D. Choose the correct words to fill in the blanks.
4. Look at Sentence J. How can we correct the mistake?
7. Look at the two sentences next to M. Which of these sentences is correct? Explain.

Conjunctive Adverb Worksheet

• conjunctive adverbs __	• conjunctions __	• start __	• do not start __

A. Words such as ***and, but,*** and ***so*** are called _____

B. **Rule 1:** Conjunctions join two sentences. They usually _____ sentences.

C. Words such as ***Therefore***, ***Moreover***, and ***However*** are called _____

D. **Rule 2:** Conjunctive adverbs usually _____ sentences.

• Therefore __	• In addition __	• Nevertheless __	• Also __	• Thus __
• As a result __	• Furthermore __	• However __	• Moreover __	

E. Conjunctive adverbs that mean the same as ***and***: _____, _____, _____, _____

F. Conjunctive adverbs that mean the same as ***but***: _____, _____

G. Conjunctive adverbs that mean the same as ***so***: _____, _____, _____

, (comma) __	**;** (semi-colon) __	**.** (period) __

H. **Rule 3:** Before a *conjunction*, we usually put a _____

I. **Rule 4:** Before a c*onjunctive adverb*, we usually put a _____ or a _____

J. The thief stole a car. But the police caught him.

K. We played soccer for four hours, therefore, our muscles hurt the next day.

L. In the course, students learned how to read a new language and tutors helped them practice it after class.

M. [1]He told me it was a secret. So, I can't tell you.
[2]He told me it was a secret. Therefore, I can't tell you.

N. [1]At the bank, I didn't have any identification, but the clerk cashed my check.
[2]At the bank, I didn't have any identification, however, the clerk cashed my check.

O. [1]Before leaving on his vacation, Tom bought a new lock for his door; in addition, he told his neighbors about his departure.
[2]Before leaving on his vacation, Tom bought a new lock for his door, in addition, he told his neighbors about his departure.

Directions

Read these directions and questions about the worksheet below to your partners.

2. Look at Sentences E though G. Choose the correct words to fill in the blanks.
5. Look at Sentence K. How can we correct the mistake?
8. Look at the two sentences next to N. Which of these sentences is correct? Explain.

Conjunctive Adverb Worksheet

> • conjunctive adverbs __   • conjunctions __   • start __   • do not start __

A. Words such as ***and, but,*** and ***so*** are called _____

B. **Rule 1:** Conjunctions join two sentences. They usually _____ sentences.

C. Words such as ***Therefore***, ***Moreover***, and ***However*** are called _____

D. **Rule 2:** Conjunctive adverbs usually _____ sentences.

> • Therefore __   • In addition __   • Nevertheless __   • Also __   • Thus __
> • As a result __   • Furthermore __   • However __   • Moreover __

E. Conjunctive adverbs that mean the same as ***and***: _____, _____,
   _____, _____

F. Conjunctive adverbs that mean the same as ***but***: _____, _____

G. Conjunctive adverbs that mean the same as ***so***: _____, _____,
   _____

> **,** (comma) __   **;** (semi-colon) __   **.** (period) __

H. **Rule 3:** Before a *conjunction*, we usually put a _____

I. **Rule 4:** Before a *conjunctive adverb*, we usually put a _____ or a _____

J. The thief stole a car. But the police caught him.

K. We played soccer for four hours, therefore, our muscles hurt the next day.

L. In the course, students learned how to read a new language and tutors helped them practice it after class.

M. [1]He told me it was a secret. So, I can't tell you.
   [2]He told me it was a secret. Therefore, I can't tell you.

N. [1]At the bank, I didn't have any identification, but the clerk cashed my check.
   [2]At the bank, I didn't have any identification, however, the clerk cashed my check.

O. [1]Before leaving on his vacation, Tom bought a new lock for his door; in addition, he told his neighbors about his departure.
   [2]Before leaving on his vacation, Tom bought a new lock for his door, in addition, he told his neighbors about his departure.

Directions

Read these directions and questions about the worksheet below to your partners.

3. Look at Sentences H through I. Choose the correct words to complete the rules.
6. Look at Sentence L. Do we need to add a comma or a period? Explain.
9. Look at Sentence O. Which of these sentences is correct? Explain.

Conjunctive Adverb Worksheet

- conjunctive adverbs __   • conjunctions __   • start __   • do not start __

A. Words such as **and, but,** and **so** are called _____
B. **Rule 1:** Conjunctions join two sentences. They usually _____ sentences.
C. Words such as **Therefore**, **Moreover**, and **However** are called _____
D. **Rule 2:** Conjunctive adverbs usually _____ sentences.

- Therefore __   • In addition __   • Nevertheless __   • Also __   • Thus __
- As a result __   • Furthermore __   • However __   • Moreover __

E. Conjunctive adverbs that mean the same as **and**: _____, _____, _____, _____
F. Conjunctive adverbs that mean the same as **but**: _____, _____
G. Conjunctive adverbs that mean the same as **so**: _____, _____, _____

- **,** (comma) __   **;** (semi-colon) __   **.** (period) __

H. **Rule 3:** Before a *conjunction*, we usually put a _____
I. **Rule 4:** Before a *conjunctive adverb*, we usually put a _____ or a _____

J. The thief stole a car. But the police caught him.
K. We played soccer for four hours, therefore, our muscles hurt the next day.
L. In the course, students learned how to read a new language and tutors helped them practice it after class.

M. [1] He told me it was a secret. So, I can't tell you.
   [2] He told me it was a secret. Therefore, I can't tell you.

N. [1] At the bank, I didn't have any identification, but the clerk cashed my check.
   [2] At the bank, I didn't have any identification, however, the clerk cashed my check.

O. [1] Before leaving on his vacation, Tom bought a new lock for his door; in addition, he told his neighbors about his departure
   [2] Before leaving on his vacation, Tom bought a new lock for his door, in addition, he told his neighbors about his departure.

Conjunctive Adverbs and Conjunctions

Exercise 1:

❶. Write **Right** next to the sentences that use commas, periods and semi-colons correctly.

❷. Write **Wrong** next to the ones that use commas, periods and semi-colons incorrectly.

_____ 1. Ken isn't good in Math. Therefore, he often has problems.

_____ 2. Ken isn't good in Math. So, he often has problems.

_____ 3. I got a library card, however, I couldn't find the book that I wanted.

_____ 4. I got a library card, but I couldn't find the book that I wanted.

_____ 5. Before his trip, Tim got a passport, in addition, he made a plane reservation.

_____ 6. Before his trip, Tim got a passport, and he made a plane reservation.

_____ 7. My father's business was doing very well; as a result, we took an expensive vacation.

_____ 8. My father's business was doing very well; so we took an expensive vacation.

Exercise 2: Circle the correct words.

1. Sue took a lot of money on her vacation. [In addition, / However,] she didn't have enough to pay for a first-class hotel.

2. My brother quit his job; [also, / nevertheless,] he moved to a new city.

3. The water in the lake looked dirty. [Moreover, / As a result,] we decided not to swim in it.

Exercise 3: Complete the sentences.

1. On the bus, I had to stand because there were no seats. Therefore, _____
   _____

2. After my rich aunt died, I inherited a house from her. Furthermore, _____
   _____

3. It was a warm sunny day yesterday. However, _____
   _____

4. It was a warm sunny day yesterday. Thus, _____
   _____

Exercise 4: Write four sentences. Use one of these words in each sentence.

| • so __ | • but __ | • Moreover __ | • As a result __ |

_____

_____

_____

_____

Unit 14

Articles (*a*, *an*, *the*)

Exercise 1: Fill in the blanks with a, an or the.

1. We saw _____ dog in the park. I got scared when _____ dog ran up to me.
2. Last year, he took _____ long trip. During _____ trip, he had several interesting experiences.
3. After graduating, Don decided to work for _____ computer company. _____ company offered him a large salary.

Exercise 2: Fill in the blanks of Rules 1 & 2 with *a, an*, or *the*.

> **Rule 1:** The first time that a noun is mentioned, we use the article "_____" or "_____" before it.
> **Rule 2:** After the first time that a noun is mentioned, we use the article "_____" before it.

Exercise 3:

❶. Double-underline the article "the" in these sentences.
❷. Underline the nouns after "the" in these sentences.
❸. Complete Rule 3 in the box below.

Sentence 1. Jack got into his car. First, he turned on the radio.
   (*Note about Sentence 1: It is clear that the radio that he turned on was his car's radio.*)

Sentence 2. I didn't sleep well last night because the phone kept ringing.
   (*Note about Sentence 2: It is clear that the phone that rang was my home phone.*)

Sentence 3. If you have problems, you should call the police immediately.
   (*Note about Sentence 3: It is obvious that you should call the police near you.*)

Sentence 4. After class, they usually spend time in the library.
   (*Note about Sentence 4: It is obvious that they study at a nearby library.*)

> **Rule 3:** If it is clear/obvious which thing/item we are talking about because of the situation, we use the article "_____" before it.

Exercise 4:

❶. Double-underline the article "the" in these sentences.
❷. Circle the adjectives that come after the articles.
❸. Underline nouns that come after the adjectives.
❹. Complete Rule 4 in the box below.

1. The best hotel that I ever stayed in was in Asia.
2. My brother got the same score as I did.
3. You finished the first step, so now you should do the next one.
4. Jim is the fastest reader in his class.

> **Rule 4:** We use the article "_____" before an adjective that shows a rank.

Exercise 4: Write articles in the blanks.

Trip to Australia (Part 1)

Last month, Tom took _____ trip to Australia. On _____ first day, he visited _____ nature park. There, he saw _____ world's deadliest spider. _____ nature park also had many crocodiles, snakes and dingoes. One of _____ crocodiles was 26 feet long. Tom also visited _____ beautiful beach. He had to be careful because _____ previous year, _____ beaches had had a problem with sharks. Therefore, he stayed near _____ shore.

Exercise 5: Insert "the" in five places (a total of six) and insert "a" in thee places.

Trip to Australia (Part 2)

That night was very hot, so Tom spent $\overset{the}{\wedge}$ time in his hotel room with air conditioner on. Next day, violent storm came. That was a little frightening. On plane going home, Tom was able to get seat next to window. Pilot explained to everyone what they could see as they were flying over Australia. Surprisingly, Tom was able to see same nature park that he had visited earlier.

Exercise 6: Insert articles.

Trip to Australia (Part 3)

From Australia, plane continued to Hawaii. Hawaii is beautiful island. As plane approached island, Tom saw beautiful beach. Beach was probably Waikiki. There were many people on beach.

Unit 15

What and *Which*

***What* introduces a noun clause.** *what* = the thing that • Noun clauses do not describe nouns. • Noun clauses do not describe verbs. **Examples:** • *I don't believe* <u>**what** he said</u>. <small>verb noun clause</small> • *He realizes* <u>**what** he did</u> *was a mistake.* <small>verb noun clause</small>	**Which introduces a relative clause.** • Relative clauses describe nouns. **Examples:** • *We need a car* <u>**which** has four doors</u>. <small>noun relative clause</small> • *She likes a place* <u>**which** has a beach</u>. <small>noun relative clause</small> • *The book* <u>**which** Ann likes</u> *is about Africa.* <small>noun relative clause</small>

Exercise 1:

   ❶. Fill in the blanks with *what* or *which*.

   ❷. In the sentences with "which," double-underline the noun that the clause describes.

1. He prefers to buy running <u>shoes</u> *which* are cheap.

2. I noticed _____ the trouble was.

3. The bike _____ is parked in the corner has a flat tire.

4. Do you know _____ the teacher assigned for homework?

5. She worries about _____ she will do in the future.

6. I am happy that the problem _____ I had was solved.

7. After the game, our team had a meeting _____ lasted for two hours.

8. We believed _____ she told us was important.

What can come after a **noun** (indirect object), but it <u>does not</u> describe that noun.

- *I asked <u>my father</u> **what** I should do.* (*"what I should do"* <u>does not</u> describe *my father*)
  indirect object

- *He showed <u>the boss</u> what the problem was.* (*"what the problem was"* <u>does not</u> describe *the boss*)
  indirect object

Exercise 2: Answer these questions about the sentences.

1. Dan told Jane <u>what we did last night</u>.
   Question: Does "what we did last night" describe Jane? _____

2. Dan told Jane about the party <u>which we will have at my apartment</u>.
   Question: Does "which we will have at my apartment" describe the party? _____

Exercise 3:

❶. Fill in the blanks with what or which.
❷. In the sentences with "which," <u>double</u>-underline the noun that the clause describes.

1. They saw the <u>car</u> *which* caused the accident.

2. They saw _____ caused the accident.

3. I told her _____ she should bring on the trip.

4. I told her about the things _____ she should bring on the trip.

5. Because we were late, he wondered _____ took us so long.

6. We put out the fire _____ had caused a lot of damage.

7. Tom gave Sue _____ she had asked him for.

8. Tom gave Sue the money _____ she had asked him for.

Exercise 4:

❶. Write <u>two sentences</u> with **what** and <u>two sentences</u> with **which**.
❷. In the sentences with "**which**," <u>double</u>-underline the noun that the clause describes.

_____

_____

_____

_____

Unit 16

Periods and Commas

Directions

Read these directions and questions about the worksheet below to your partners.

1. In Sentence A , underline the conjunction. (If you need help, look at Unit 2)
4. In Sentence A, circle the comma.
7. In Sentence B , write V above the verb that is <u>after</u> the conjunction.
10. In Sentence C, do we need a comma in this sentence?
13. In Sentence E, how can we improve this?
16. Can you explain why we need a comma in Sentence G but not in Sentence H?
19. In Sentences K and L, underline the dependent clause.
22. In Sentences M and N, underline the dependent clause.
25. In Sentence O, where do we need a comma or period?

Periods and Commas Worksheet

A. I like Fridays, but Sam prefers Saturdays.

B. He finished his work and went home.

C. She felt sick so she left work early.

D. They talked about their vacation plans they didn't go to bed until 2 a.m.

E. Summer is my favorite season. But New Year's is my favorite holiday.

F. The employer paid women less money. Therefore, many of them quit.

G. Because it is snowing, we'll be able to go skiing.

H. We'll be able to go skiing because it is snowing.

I. He has a great job, however he plans to quit in two years in order to travel.

J. Twice a week, she runs for exercise. Furthermore on weekends, she goes to the pool.

K. Ann studied French before she went to France.

L. Before Ann went to France, she studied French.

M. After he had solved the problem, he went to bed.

N. He went to bed after he had solved the problem.

O. Jim is afraid of snakes as a result he doesn't like the desert.

Directions

Read these directions and questions about the worksheet below to your partners.

2. In Sentence A, write S above the subject and V above the verb that are <u>before</u> the conjunction.
5. In Sentence B, underline the conjunction.
8. In Sentence B, is there a comma?
11. In Sentence D, do we need to add a comma or period? Why?
14. In Sentence F, are the period and comma used correctly? (If you need help, see Unit 2)
17. In Sentence I, are there any comma problems here?
20. In Sentences K and L, circle any commas that you find.
23. In Sentences M and N, circle any commas.

Periods and Commas Worksheet

A. I like Fridays, but Sam prefers Saturdays.

B. He finished his work and went home.

C. She felt sick so she left work early.

D. They talked about their vacation plans they didn't go to bed until 2 a.m.

E. Summer is my favorite season. But New Year's is my favorite holiday.

F. The employer paid women less money. Therefore, many of them quit.

G. Because it is snowing, we'll be able to go skiing.

H. We'll be able to go skiing because it is snowing.

I. He has a great job, however he plans to quit in two years in order to travel.

J. Twice a week, she runs for exercise. Furthermore on weekends, she goes to the pool.

K. Ann studied French before she went to France.

L. Before Ann went to France, she studied French.

M. After he had solved the problem, he went to bed.

N. He went to bed after he had solved the problem.

O. Jim is afraid of snakes as a result he doesn't like the desert.

Directions

Read these directions and questions about the worksheet below to your partners.

3. In Sentence A , write S above the subject and V above the verb that are <u>after</u> the conjunction.

6. In Sentence B, write S above the subject and V above the verb that are <u>before</u> the conjunction.

9. In Sentence B, why don't we use a comma in this sentence?

12. In Sentence D, if I want to put a comma, should I also add a conjunction?

15. In Sentences G and H, circle any commas.

18. In Sentence J, do we need a comma after the word "Furthermore"?

21. Why is there a comma in Sentence L but not in Sentence K?

24. Why is there a comma in Sentence M but not in Sentence N?

Periods and Commas Worksheet

A. I like Fridays, but Sam prefers Saturdays.

B. He finished his work and went home.

C. She felt sick so she left work early.

D. They talked about their vacation plans they didn't go to bed until 2 a.m.

E. Summer is my favorite season. But New Year's is my favorite holiday.

F. The employer paid women less money. Therefore, many of them quit.

G. Because it is snowing, we'll be able to go skiing.

H. We'll be able to go skiing because it is snowing.

I. He has a great job, however he plans to quit in two years in order to travel.

J. Twice a week, she runs for exercise. Furthermore on weekends, she goes to the pool.

K. Ann studied French before she went to France.

L. Before Ann went to France, she studied French.

M. After he had solved the problem, he went to bed.

N. He went to bed after he had solved the problem.

O. Jim is afraid of snakes as a result he doesn't like the desert.

Unit 17
Periods and Commas

Exercise 1:

❶. Look at the examples.
❷. For **Rules 1** and **2**, fill in the blanks with the correct word from the box.

• period __   • independent clause __   • comma __ • comma __ • comma __
• conjunctive adverbs __   • subject __   • dependent clause __   • conjunction __

Examples for **Rules 1** and **2**

1. The <u>meat</u>ˢ was old, **so** <u>we</u>ˢ threw it away.

2. His <u>father</u>ˢ gave him a computer, **and** his **brother**ˢ bought him a printer for his graduation.

3. <u>Tom</u>ˢ washed the car <u>and cleaned</u> the garage.

(Choose words from the box at the top of the page to fill in the blanks.)

Rule 1: Put a *comma* before a _____ if the sentence has a <u>subject</u> <u>before</u> and a <u>subject</u> <u>after</u> the conjunction.

Rule 2: Do not put a comma if there is no _____ after the conjunction.

Examples for **Rule 3**

4. I own a car . However , the battery is dead.
5. They had an argument . Therefore , they decided to see a counselor.

(Choose words from the box at the top of the page to fill in the blanks.)

Rule 3: Put a _____ before a _____ and put a _____ after it.

---

6. <u>When Dan woke up</u> **,** he noticed the sunlight.

7. <u>Before she saw the movie</u> **,** Jane read the book.

8. He went to the dentist <u>as soon as his tooth began to hurt</u>.

9. You should call me <u>if you need any help</u>.

(Choose words from the box at the top of page 179 to fill in the blanks.)

Rule 4: If a sentence starts with a _____, put a _____ after it.

Rule 5: If a sentence starts with an _____, do not use a comma.

Exercise 2:

❶. **Double**-underline the conjunction. *(If you need help, see Unit 12.)*

❷. Put in commas if they are needed.

1. His father likes golf and his mother enjoys tennis.
2. Don drinks coffee in the morning and has tea in the afternoon.
3. Jack traveled around Europe and wrote a book, before getting a job for a newspaper.
4. By working in the library, Sara learned about computers and she was able to meet some interesting people.

Exercise 3:

❶. Double-underline the conjunctive adverbs. *(If you need help, see Unit 12.)*

❷. Put in commas and periods if they are needed.

1. We found a great house to buy However the price was too high.
2. John got a new pair of glasses Therefore he was able to pass his driving test easily.

Exercise 4:

❶. Underline the dependent clause. *(If you need help, see Unit 6.)*

❷. Put in commas if they are needed.

1. I started coughing because he was smoking a cigarette.
2. Because he was smoking a cigarette I started coughing.
3. After the child got his toy he stopped crying.
4. If you don't hurry we'll be late for the start of the movie.
5. Ken drove the car while Steve studied the map.

Exercise 5: Put in commas if they are needed.

1. When you are shopping you should try to find some bargains.
2. Jan likes to collect seashells and make necklaces from them.
3. One of my brothers lives in the city and the other one lives on a farm.
4. I like the tune of the first song but hate the second one.
5. They should go to the beach if they want to see a spectacular sunset.
6. When a storm comes you should close the windows. Also it's a good idea to turn off the computer.

Unit 18
Conditional *"If"* Sentences

If + present, future

- This means there is a good chance that this situation will happen in the future.

Example:

- If I <u>pass</u> this class, I <u>will be</u> happy.
  present   future

If + past, *(would* + verb)

- The situation is not true, or there is little chance that it will happen.

Example:

- *I speak only English. If I <u>spoke</u> French, I <u>would visit</u> Paris.*
  past   would + verb

(Note: **Never** write *"If + was."* The correct form is *"If + were.")*
Examples: *If I* **were** *sick, I would call you. If he* **were** *older, he would work here.*

Exercise 1:

❶. Underline the verb that is given.

❷. Fill in the blanks with the correct verb tense of the other verb.

1. If he <u>brings</u> his guitar to the party, he *will play* (to play) it for us.

2. If you get up late, you _____ (to miss) your bus.

3. If my grandparents were alive, they _____ (to live) with us.

4. If I _____ (to buy) that new CD, I will let you borrow it.

5. If we _____ (to have) a new battery, we would use it in this flashlight.

6. He _____ (to save) more money if he didn't have an expensive hobby.

7. On the long trip, our children _____ (to not be) bored if they have some toys.

8. I _____ (to not want) a large car if I had to drive it in a large city.

9. If she _____ (to be) a better actress, she would star in more movies.

Exercise 2:

Rewrite these sentences indicating that the situation is **not true**.

1. If I have enough money, I will buy a car.
2. If I buy a car, I'll get an SUV.
3. If I get an SUV, I'll drive to Denver.
4. If I drive to Denver, I'll visit Dave.
5. If I visit Dave, we'll go camping.
6. If we go camping, we'll hike in the mountains.
7. If we hike in the mountains, we'll see a bear.
8. If we see a bear, we'll be scared.
9. If we're scared, we will run very fast.
10. If we run fast enough, we'll escape.

1. *If I had enough money, I would buy a car.* _____
2. _____
3. _____
4. _____
5. _____
6. _____
7. _____
8. _____
9. _____
10. _____
11. *If we escaped,* _____
   (finish the story.)

Exercise 3: Complete the sentences using the correct verb form.

1. If he had a pet in his home now, _____
2. If we have time tonight, _____
3. I will celebrate if _____
4. I would celebrate if _____

Exercise 4: Write four more sentences about yourself using "if."

_____
_____
_____
_____

Unit 19

Adjectives

Common adjectives

- slow __   - beautiful __   - poor __   - fast __   - easy __   - terrible __

Exercise 1:

❶. Write **V** above the verbs.

❷. Fill in the blanks with some of the adjectives from the box above.

1. This job is ___*easy*___ .
   ^v — (V above "is")

2. When I was in high school, I was a _____ runner. I won many races.

3. She couldn't sleep because the storm was _____.

4. The people in the town were _____, so they couldn't afford to pay for medicine.

Common mistake: No Verb

(mistake) She <u>interested</u> in music.

(correct) She <u>is</u> interested in music.

Adjectives that are often incorrectly used as verbs

• afraid	• angry	• confused	• disappointed
• embarrassed	• excited	• frightened	• glad
• interested	• proud	• satisfied	• shocked
• surprised	• sorry	• tired	• upset

Exercise 2:

❶. Write V above the verbs that come before the adjectives.

❷. Fill in the blanks with adjectives from the box above.

1. At the end of the day, I felt _____ from working so hard.

2. When he arrived, he was _____ that his wife was having a party for him.

3. The child became _____ because there was a large dog running toward him.

4. I couldn't find my friend's house because I got _____ by his directions.

Exercise 3:

❶. If the underlined part of the sentence is correct, write **OK**. (There are two of these.)

❷. If the underlined part of the sentence is not correct, change it.

Ann was disappointed

_____ 1. <u>Ann disappointed</u> that her team lost.

_____ 2. After he got the report, <u>he looked happy</u>.

_____ 3. My brother got a new house, and now <u>he satisfied</u> with it.

_____ 4. <u>The tourists angry</u> that the plane was delayed.

_____ 5. <u>He was sorry</u> to learn that she didn't get a date.

_____ 6. When the dentist told him that he needed to have a tooth pulled, <u>he upset</u>.

_____ 7. <u>He shocked</u> to learn that he had lost his job.

A *less common* pattern: S + V + person

S   V   person
He <u>surprised</u> his girlfriend at the restaurant.

Verbs followed by a person
(Here, all are in past tense form.)

• surprised	• frightened	• embarrassed
• disappointed	• upset	• shocked

Exercise 4:

❶. Write **V** above the verbs.

❷. Write **person** above the person after the verb.

               V   person
1. The ghost story <u>frightened</u> the <u>boys</u>.

2. His strange laugh embarrassed everyone in the room.

3. Because of his poor performance, he disappointed his coach.

4. The bad news upset my father.

5. He shocked me with the news that he was joining the army.

6. Tammy's friends surprised her with a gift.

7. It surprised Tammy when her friends gave her a gift.

Exercise 5:

❶. If the sentence is correct, write **OK**. <u>(There are four of these.)</u>
❷. If the sentence is **not** correct, change it.

1. <u>Tim is terrible</u> in Math.

2. After she graduated, <u>her parents proud of her</u>.

3. <u>It upsets John</u> when his computer crashes.

4. The <u>customers were disappointed</u> about the rising prices.

5. The shy man couldn't give his speech because <u>he embarrassed</u>.

6. <u>I often afraid</u> to drive on the expressway.

7. At the concert, the <u>singer was shocked</u> her fans when she stopped singing after only 30 minutes.

8. <u>They glad</u> that the bus arrived before the rain began.

9. When the lecture ended, I asked the speaker to explain the points that <u>I was confused</u> about.

Exercise 6: Write five sentences. Use one of these words in each sentence.

• excited __ • frightened __ • confused __ • disappointed __ • angry __

_____

_____

_____

_____

_____

Unit 20
Adverbs and Adjectives

Exercise 1: In the box, circle the adverbs. *(If you are not sure, look in a dictionary.)*

> • soft __ • quickly __ • safely __ • happily __ • surprising __ • easy __

Exercise 2: Choose words from the box to fill in the blanks.

❶. If the word describes a noun, use an adjective
❷. If the word describes a verb, use an adverb.

1. This is an _____ exercise. *("Exercise" is a noun, so we use an adjective.)*
2. He sang _____ as he worked.
3. I couldn't hear the speaker because his voice was too _____ .
4. They finished their assignments _____ , so they left early.
5. John told me the _____ news that he was moving overseas soon.

Exercise 3:

❶. For each word in the box, write whether it is an adverb or an adjective.
❷. Write three sentences using the words in the box.

> • heavy __ • quiet __ • carefully __ • bad __ • seriously __

1. *heavy (adjective): I hurt my back lifting a heavy table.* _____
2. _____
3. _____
4. _____

Exercise 4: Some **adjectives** end in **-ly**.
  Write Correct next to the sentences that use the underlined word correctly.

_____ 1. After moving to the city, I was <u>lonely</u>.

_____ 2. My roommate left, so I watched TV *lonely*.

_____ 3. <u>Elderly</u> people are often very wise.

_____ 4. When he returned from the hospital, my father walked <u>elderly</u>.

_____ 5. She sang <u>lovely</u> during the concert.

_____ 6. She sang a <u>lovely</u> song during the concert.

Exercise 5: Some words can be both **adverbs** and **adjectives**: *fast, hard, late.*

❶. Write **Adjective** in the blank if the underlined word is an adjective.
❷. Write **Adverb** in the blank if the underlined word is an adverb.

_____ 1. We took a <u>fast</u> train into the city.

_____ 2. My brother got a ticket because he drove too <u>fast</u>.

_____ 3. You can improve if you work <u>hard</u>.

_____ 4. I stayed up late because I had a <u>hard</u> assignment to finish.

Exercise 6:

❶. Write a sentence with *late* used as an **adverb**.
❷. Write a sentence with *late* used as an **adjective**.

1. _____

2. _____

Exercise 7: Write *hard* and *hardly* in the blanks.

┌───┐
│   • *hardly* (adverb) = not very much   │
│   • *hard*   (adverb) = with effort   │
└───┘

_____ 1. I'm very tired because I worked _____ yesterday.

_____ 2. I'm not tired because I _____ did any work yesterday.

_____ 3. The reason that she failed the test was because she _____ studied.

_____ 4. She got the best score in the class because she had studied _____ .

Exercise 8: Adverbs tell us **when, where, how** and **how often.**
In the blanks, write what the underlined adverb tells us.

*when*___ 1. I returned home from my vacation yesterday.

_____ 2. You need to sit here if you are waiting to use the Internet.

_____ 3. Tom always looks at a map before he starts a trip.

_____ 4. After the accident, Ann carefully got out of the car.

_____ 5. Sue checks her e-mail messages regularly.

_____ 6. Now, we'll take a break.

Exercise 9:

❶. Underline the adverbs.

❷. Write what the adverb tells us: *when, where, how* or *how often.*

how often 1. Steve is afraid of flying, so he <u>rarely</u> travels by plane.

_____ 2. We wrote our names there.

_____ 3. When the packages arrived, Dan quickly opened them.

_____ 4. Tomorrow, we plan to pay our taxes.

_____ 5. Ken drove the car well.

_____ 6. Jim has never visited Africa.

_____ 7. They will soon learn who told the secret.

Exercise 10: Adverbs can be used as *intensifiers* <u>before an adjective or adverb</u>.

Intensifiers
• very __   • rather __   • quite __   • terribly __   • extremely __

❶. <u>Double</u>-underline the intensifier.

❷. Underline the adjective or adverb that comes after the intensifier.

❸. Write **adj** (adjective) or **adv** (adverb) above the words that you underlined.

                            adj
1. After eating the food, she became <u>rather</u> sick.

2. I read all his novels because he is a very good writer.

3. Very often, we are confused by his behavior.

4. She became extremely rich after winning the lottery.

5. The child fell into the river, but very luckily, someone rescued him.

6. My brother arrived home terribly late, so my parents were angry.

7. I am quite hungry.

Exercise 11:

❶. Write **adj** above the underlined word if it is an adjective.
❷. Write **adv** above the underlined word if it is an adverb.
❸. Write **int** above the underlined word if it is an intensifier.

1. Tom <u>slowly</u> picked up the <u>expensive</u> statue.

2. Jim could <u>hardly</u> stay awake because he was <u>so</u> tired, but <u>later</u> he felt better.

3. When Jane lived in the city, she could <u>easily</u> find <u>very</u> <u>inexpensive</u> clothes.

4. There were only a <u>few</u> minutes left, so I had to read <u>extremely</u> <u>fast</u>.

5. <u>Yesterday</u>, while I was trying to study <u>hard</u>, a dog kept barking because he was <u>lonely</u>.

Adverbs and Adjectives

Directions

Read these directions and questions <u>about the worksheet below</u> to your partners.

1. In Sentence A , is "fast" an adverb or an adjective.
4. In Sentence B, do we need a comma?
7. In Sentence E, there is a problem with the word "confused"? Explain.
10. In G, write a sentence using the word "embarrassed" as an adjective.
13. In Sentence I, is the word "question" a noun or a verb?
16. In Sentence J, is the word "drove" a noun or a verb?
19. In Sentence K, circle the adverb.
22. In Sentence M, explain the problem with the word "hardly."
25. In Sentence P, underline the adverb.
28. In Sentence Q, what does the adverb tell us?

Adverbs and Adjectives Worksheet

A. He ran very fast.

B. They would sleep in a tent if they <u>went</u> on a trip.

C. She easy answered all the hard questions.

D. My sister is wonderful.

E. Jim confused about the rule.

F. After the waiter corrected his mistake on our bill, <u>I satisfied</u>.

G. (embarrassed) _____

H. (embarrassed) _____

I. Sara asked a great question.

J. He drove the car recklessly.

K. During the concert, the audience sat silently and enjoyed listening to the famous musician.

L. After her roommate had left, Jane's apartment was quiet, so she felt lonely.

M. My father was happy with me because I had worked hardly all afternoon.

N. Adverbs tell us <u>when</u>, w_____, h_____, and <u>how often</u>.

O. It was sad leaving my hometown because I had lived <u>there</u> for 18 years.

P. They quickly finished washing the dishes.

Q. Bill is afraid of horses because he has never ridden one.

R. She is a very good artist.

Directions

Read these directions and questions <u>about the worksheet below</u> to your partners.

2. In Sentence A, what kind of adverb is "very"?
5. In Sentence C, is there a problem with this sentence?
8. In Sentence E, put in a verb.
11. In H, write a sentence using the word "embarrassed" as a verb.
14. In Sentence I, is the word "great" an adjective or an adverb?
17. In Sentence J, is the word "recklessly" an adjective or adverb?
20. In Sentence L, how many adjectives are there?
23. In Sentence N, fill in the blanks.
26. In Sentence P, what does the adverb tell us?
29. In Sentence R, one of these words is an adverb. It is called an intensifier. Circle it.

Adverbs and Adjectives Worksheet

A. He ran very fast.

B. They would sleep in a tent if they <u>went</u> on a trip.

C. She easy answered all the hard questions.

D. My sister is wonderful.

E. Jim confused about the rule.

F. After the waiter corrected his mistake on our bill, <u>I satisfied</u>.

G. (embarrassed) _____

H. (embarrassed) _____

I. Sara asked a great question.

J. He drove the car recklessly.

K. During the concert, the audience sat silently and enjoyed listening to the famous musician.

L. After her roommate had left, Jane's apartment was quiet, so she felt lonely.

M. My father was happy with me because I had worked hardly all afternoon.

N. Adverbs tell us <u>when</u>, w_____, h_____, and <u>how often</u>.

O. It was sad leaving my hometown because I had lived <u>there</u> for 18 years.

P. They quickly finished washing the dishes.

Q. Bill is afraid of horses because he has never ridden one.

R. She is a very good artist.

Directions

Read these directions and questions <u>about the worksheet below</u> to your partners.

3. In Sentence B, is there a problem with the underlined verb?

6. In Sentence D, circle the adjective. (If you need help, see Unit 19)

9. In Sentence F, correct the problem.

12. In Sentence I, what word does the word "great" describe? (If you need help, see Unit 20.)

15. In Sentence J, what word does the word "recklessly" describe?

18. In Sentence K, underline the adjective.

21. In Sentence L, how many adverbs are there?

24. In Sentence O, what does the word "there" tell us?

27. In Sentence Q, underline the adverb.

Adverbs and Adjectives Worksheet

A. He ran very fast.

B. They would sleep in a tent if they <u>went</u> on a trip.

C. She easy answered all the hard questions.

D. My sister is wonderful.

E. Jim confused about the rule.

F. After the waiter corrected his mistake on our bill, <u>I satisfied</u>.

G. (embarrassed) _____

H. (embarrassed) _____

I. Sara asked a great question.

J. He drove the car recklessly.

K. During the concert, the audience sat silently and enjoyed listening to the famous musician.

L. After her roommate had left, Jane's apartment was quiet, so she felt lonely.

M. My father was happy with me because I had worked hardly all afternoon.

N. Adverbs tell us <u>when</u>, w_____, h_____, and <u>how often</u>.

O. It was sad leaving my hometown because I had lived <u>there</u> for 18 years.

P. They quickly finished washing the dishes.

Q. Bill is afraid of horses because he has never ridden one.

R. She is a very good artist.

Unit 22
Word-Choice Problems

Exercise 1: *marry* (verb), *married* (adjective), *marriage* (noun).
Write **Right** next to the four sentences that use these correctly.

_____ 1. He plans to get married when he is 22.

_____ 2. He plans to get marry when he is 22.

_____ 3. He plans to get marriage when he is 22.

_____ 4. It would be interesting to marry with a foreigner.

_____ 5. It would be interesting to marry a foreigner.

_____ 6. They were marriage in July.

_____ 7. They were marry in July.

_____ 8. They were married in July.

_____ 9. My parents' marriage has lasted 35 years.

Exercise 2: Write **Right** next to the five sentences that use the **noun forms** correctly.

_____ 1. Before our trip, we got some <u>informations</u>.

_____ 2. Before our trip, we got some <u>information</u>.

_____ 3. My hometown is surrounded by a lot of <u>nature</u>.

_____ 4. My hometown is surrounded by a lot of <u>natures</u>.

_____ 5. If you are looking for some <u>entertainment</u>, you should go downtown.

_____ 6. If you are looking for some <u>entertainments</u>, you should go downtown.

_____ 7. All the <u>pollutions</u> in the air will cause breathing problems.

_____ 8. All the <u>pollution</u> in the air will cause breathing problems.

_____ 9. There are many types of <u>transportation</u> in the city.

_____ 10. There are many types of <u>transportations</u> in the city.

Exercise 3: Write **Right** next to the one sentence that uses the correct expression.

_____ 1. <u>Most of people</u> enjoy the holidays.

_____ 2. <u>Almost people</u> enjoy the holidays.

_____ 3. <u>Most people</u> enjoy the holidays.

Exercise 4: Write **Right** next to the six sentences whose underlined sections are written correctly.

_____ 1. <u>Students</u> who speak English <u>are easy</u> to find jobs in my country.

_____ 2. <u>It is easy for students</u> who speak English to find jobs in my country.

_____ 3. <u>Jobs are easy</u> to find for students who speak English.

_____ 4. <u>It is common for old people</u> to live in a nursing home.

_____ 5. <u>Old people are common</u> to live in a nursing home.

_____ 6. <u>Nursing homes are common places</u> for old people to live.

_____ 7. <u>People are often difficult</u> to drive in a big city.

_____ 8. <u>It is often difficult</u> to drive in a big city.

_____ 9. <u>Driving is often difficult</u> in a big city.

Exercise 5: Write **Right** next to the seven sentences that use the apostrophe correctly.

_____ 1. Tom's computers are getting old.

_____ 2. Toms' computers are getting old.

_____ 3. I have two roommates. Both of my roommates' beds are a mess.

_____ 4. I have two roommates. Both of my roommate's beds are a mess.

_____ 5. I have one roommate. My roommates' bed is a mess.

_____ 6. I have one roommate. My roommate's bed is a mess.

_____ 7. Both of my parents write me. I look forward to my parents' letters.

_____ 8. Both of my parents write me. I look forward to my parent's letters.

_____ 9. All the students passed the class. In fact, the students' grades were great.

_____ 10. All the students passed the class. In fact, the student's grades were great.

_____ 11. I am looking for some mens' shoes.

_____ 12. I am looking for some men's shoes.

_____ 13. The peoples' choice for president was interesting.

_____ 14. The people's choice for president was interesting.

Exercise 6: Write eleven sentences. Each sentence should include one of the following:

- married __
- marriage __
- marry __
- information __
- pollution __
- nature __
- easy __
- difficult __
- most __
- _____'s __
- _____s' __

1. _____

2. _____

3. _____

4. _____

5. _____

6. _____

7. _____

8. _____

9. _____

10. _____

11. _____

Unit 23

Verbs followed by Gerunds or Infinitives

Exercise 1: Write the correct form (gerund or infinitive) of the verbs in parentheses.
Gerunds are <u>verb</u>-*ing (talking)* and **infinitives** are *to* + <u>verb</u> *(to talk)*.

1. She **delayed** ___*writing*___ *(write)* her report.

2. This picture **appears** ___*to be*___ *(be)* expensive.

3. She didn't get the message because we **forgot** _____ *(contact)* her.

4. I **miss** _____ *(see)* the sunrise when I sleep late in the morning.

5. I don't **enjoy** _____ *(write)* letters.

6. He **considered** _____ *(take)* the job after seeing the high salary.

7. She **seems** _____ *(be)* unhappy about the results.

8. I won't need your help because Sally already **offered** _____ *(help)* me.

9. We can take my car if you **promise** _____ *(pay)* for the gas.

10. You don't **need** _____ *(bring)* anything with you.

11. Ken is tired today because he didn't **finish** _____ *(paint)* until 2 a.m.

12. His parents **regretted** _____ *(buy)* him a motorcycle.

13. After the movie, we all **agreed** _____ *(meet)* at a restaurant.

14. If you go to London, you should **plan** _____ *(see)* some museums.

15. Most people **hope** _____ *(enjoy)* good health in the future.

16. While driving to work, Tom **practiced** _____ *(say)* his speech.

17. I told him that I didn't **mean** _____ *(laugh)* at his tie.

18. When you finish your essay, I **recommend** _____ *(read)* it again.

19. Tom **refused** _____ *(give)* me any money.

20. Because of the good price, Jane **decided** _____ *(buy)* the car.

21. He **learned** _____ *(make)* omelets from his friend.

22. I am **prepared** _____ *(find)* a new job if the boss fires me.

Exercise 2: Fill in the chart with the **bold verbs** from Exercise 1.

> ### *Verbs that are followed by a* gerund (<u>verb</u>-*ing*)
>
> • delay

> ### *Verbs that are followed by an* infinitive (*to* + <u>verb</u>)
>
> • appear

Exercise 3: Complete the sentences by including a **gerund** or **infinitive**.

1. Since I forgot _____

2. After you wash the dishes, you should finish _____

3. My sister agreed _____

4. We really don't want to visit him because he seems _____

5. After Don failed the class, he considered _____

6. They are upset at Ann because she refused _____

7. When it is warm outside, I enjoy _____

8. She didn't want to go on a date with him, so she pretended _____

9. My father wants me to practice _____

10. Before leaving the house, we decided _____

11. My best friend promised _____

12. Now that she is an adult, she misses _____

13. I plan _____

Unit 24

Prepositions

Exercise 1: Fill in the blanks with the correct prepositions from the box.

• about __	• at __	• by __	• from __	• in __
• of __	• to __	• with __	• for __	

1. This is the third time you were **absent** _____from_____ this class.

2. Dan doesn't play football because he is **afraid** _____ getting hurt.

3. He won't help because he is **angry** _____ us.

4. Their mother was **ashamed** _____ the way her children behaved.

*5. Ken is **bad** _____ tennis, but he is good _____ chess.

*6. We fell asleep because we were **bored** _____ the lecture.

7. She wants to buy a car that is **different** _____ everyone else's.

8. I couldn't sleep because I was **excited** _____ our trip.

*9. They were **happy** _____ their results.

*10. Mike was **impressed** _____ my great plan.

11. Tim is **interested** _____ making more money.

12. Sara would like to get **married** _____ someone older than her.

13. We were **nervous** _____ riding in the car while Steve was driving.

14. Without a doubt, Bill was **ready** _____ a vacation.

*15. You shouldn't feel **upset** _____ your salary.

*16. They were **satisfied** _____ his explanation.

17. Sue couldn't finish the letter on time because she is **slow** _____ writing.

*18. I am **sorry** _____ your troubles.

19. Jim was **tired** _____ waiting, so he left.

   * *In these sentences, two different prepositions are possible with these adjectives.*

Exercise 2: Complete the sentences. Include a preposition after the adjective.

1. Before going to school, Jane was nervous _____

2. As a child, I was bad _____, but I was
   good _____

3. These days, I am satisfied _____, but I am
   worried _____

4. She was tired _____, so she decided to go outside.

5. If you visit my country, you will be impressed _____

Unit 25

Review of Phrases and Clauses

Directions

Read these directions and questions about the worksheet below to your partners.

1. In A, is this a phrase or a clause? How do you know? *(If you need help, see Unit 6.)*
4. In C, is this a phrase or a clause? How do you know?
7. In E, underline any independent clauses that you see.
10. In F, circle the dependent clause.
13. In G, underline any independent clauses that you see.
16. In G, how can we correct this?
19. In H, is this called a run-on, a comma splice or a fragment?
22. In I, is this called a run-on, a comma splice or a fragment?
25. In J, do we need a comma?
28. In K, do we need a comma?
31. In L, do we need a comma?

Phrases and Clauses Worksheet

A. they saw a great view from the top of the building

B. on the ship

C. After we visited the museum.

D. My mother, who likes flowers, spends a lot of time in the garden.

E. He checked the Internet. He found the best airfare.

F. Sara got her passport. Before she left on her trip.

G. Ken went to the market his wife stayed home.

H. We enjoy tea, they prefer drinking coffee.

I. While we were waiting for the train.

J. His watch stopped so he didn't know the time.

K. After Jim won the game he was very satisfied.

L. Jane gave some money to a charity because she is a generous person.

Directions

Read these directions and questions about the worksheet below to your partners.

2. In A, is this a dependent or independent clause?

5. In C, is this a dependent or independent clause? How do we know?

8. In E, can we have a period between 2 independent clauses?

11. In F, is there a problem? Explain.

14. In G, can we put 2 independent clauses together like this?

17. In H, underline any independent clauses that you see.

20. In H, how can we correct this?

23. In I, how can we correct this?

26. In K, circle the dependent clause.

29. In L, circle the dependent clause.

Phrases and Clauses Worksheet

A. they saw a great view from the top of the building

B. on the ship

C. After we visited the museum.

D. My mother, who likes flowers, spends a lot of time in the garden.

E. He checked the Internet. He found the best airfare.

F. Sara got her passport. Before she left on her trip.

G. Ken went to the market his wife stayed home.

H. We enjoy tea, they prefer drinking coffee.

 I. While we were waiting for the train.

J. His watch stopped so he didn't know the time.

K. After Jim won the game he was very satisfied.

L. Jane gave some money to a charity because she is a generous person.

Directions

Read these directions and questions about the worksheet below to your partners.

3. In B, is this a phrase or a clause? How do we know?

6. In D, circle the dependent clause.

9. In F, underline the independent clause.

12. In F, how can we correct this?

15. In G, is this called a run-on, a comma splice or a fragment?

18. In H, can we put 2 independent clauses together with a comma like this?

21. In I, is this a dependent or independent clause?

24. In J, can we combine 2 independent clauses with the word "so."

27. In K, underline the independent clause.

30. In L, underline the independent clause.

Phrases and Clauses Worksheet

A. they saw a great view from the top of the building

B. on the ship

C. After we visited the museum.

D. My mother, who likes flowers, spends a lot of time in the garden.

E. He checked the Internet. He found the best airfare.

F. Sara got her passport. Before she left on her trip.

G. Ken went to the market his wife stayed home.

H. We enjoy tea, they prefer drinking coffee.

I. While we were waiting for the train.

J. His watch stopped so he didn't know the time.

K. After Jim won the game he was very satisfied.

L. Jane gave some money to a charity because she is a generous person.

Unit 26
-ing/-ed Adjectives

> **Usually:**
> ***Things*** are *-ing* (The <u>book</u> is **interesting**. This is an **exciting** <u>movie</u>.)
> ***People*** are *-ed* (<u>Ken</u> is **interested** in snowboarding. His <u>parents</u> were **worried**.)

Exercise 1: Write the correct form of the adjective (*-ing* or *-ed*).

1. *(disappoint)* The boy felt ___*disappointed*___ about his grade.
2. *(bore)* Jane thinks that her job is _____. She is _____.
3. *(surprise)* The news was very surprising, but not everyone was_____.
4. *(amaze)* Computer technology is _____ these days.
5. *(embarrass)* He gets _____ when he has to give a speech.
6. *(tire)* I am _____ of washing dishes every night.
7. *(bore)* The reason Don hates weekends is because he is always _____.
8. *(confuse/confuse)* The teacher's directions were _____. As a result, the students felt _____ about the assignments.
9. *(satisfy)* The police were _____ with my explanation of what had happened.
10. *(annoy)* He could not sleep well because he felt _____ by his roommate.
11. *(frighten)* She started to scream when she saw a _____ scene in the movie.
12. *(disappoint)* After hearing the _____ news, I decided to cancel my plan. Of course, I was very disappointed.

Exercise 2:

❶. Write six sentences. Use one of these words with each sentence:

   • bored __   • boring __   • excited __   • exciting __   • interested __   • interesting __

❷. Underline the person or thing that is described.

1. _____

2. _____

3. _____

4. _____

5. _____

6. _____

Unit 27

Comparisons

Exercise 1: Fill in the blanks with the words from the box.

• much __	• the __	• as __

❶. *Wrong:* He is _as same age as_ me.

  Correct: He is _____ same age **as** me.

❷. *Wrong:* We worked _as possible as_ we could.

  Correct: We worked _____ _____ **as** possible.

Patterns

• *the same* <u>noun</u> *as* _____	• *as* <u>adjective</u> *as* _____
• Sara lives in **the same** <u>city</u> **as** Jane.	• Bill is **as** <u>strong</u> **as** his brother.
• They study **the same** <u>book</u> **as** we do.	• They study **as** <u>much</u> **as** we do.
	• They study **as** <u>much</u> **as** possible.

Exercise 2:

❶. Write **noun** or **adj** (adjective) next to the word.

❷. Write a sentence using the pattern.

1. She was born in 1980. He was born in 1980.
   (**age:** *noun*) She is the same **age** as him.
   (**old:** *adj*) She is as **old** as him.

2. This red bike is $150. That blue bike is $150.
   (**price:** _____) _____
   (**expensive:** _____) _____

3. Bill is 178 pounds. Sam is 178 pounds.
   (**heavy:** _____) _____
   (**weight:** _____) _____

4. Our school has 500 students. Their school has 500 students.
   (**size:** _____) _____ *(Hint: use "is.")*
   (**big:** _____) _____ *(Hint: use "is.")*

5. My essay is two pages long. Your essay is two pages long.
   (**long:** _____) _____
   (**length:** _____) _____

6. Joe is 6 feet tall. Ted is 6 feet tall.
   (**height:** _____) _____
   (**tall:** _____) _____

Exercise 3:

❶. Write **noun** or **adj** (adjective) next to the word in the box.

❷. Write four more sentences. In each sentence use one of the words in the box below and one of the patterns in the box on page 202.

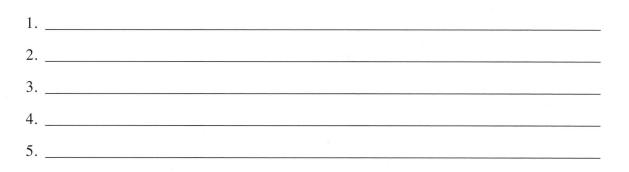

1. serious *adj* 2. hard _____ 3. hometown _____ 4. computer _____ 5. beautiful _____

1. *Joe is as serious as I am.* _____
2. _____
3. _____
4. _____
5. _____

Exercise 4: Using comparisons, write five sentences about your family or your country.

1. _____
2. _____
3. _____
4. _____
5. _____

Unit 28

Passive Voice
Directions

Read these directions and questions <u>about the worksheet below</u> to your partners.

1. In Sentence A, write S above the subject and V above the verb.
4. In Sentence B, circle the words "by my brother."
7. In Sentence D, change Sentence C to passive by filling in the blanks.
   Also, write the word "passive" in the blank after it.
10. I'll dictate H. Fill in the blanks with this: Auxiliary *be* includes *is, are, was, were, being, been.*
13. In Sentence K, write the word "be" above the auxiliary *be*.
16. In L, change the sentence to passive.
19. In N, change the sentence to passive.

Passive Voice Worksheet

A. My brother helped me. (_____)

B. I was helped by my brother. (_____)

C. His girlfriend made him this sweater. (_____)

D. _____ was made by _____. (_____)

E. Those boys broke the window. (active)

F. The window _____ _____ by those boys. (passive)

G. Passive verb uses auxiliary *be* + _____ _____.

H. Auxiliary **be** includes *is,* _____, _____, *were,* _____ _____.

I. Past participles of verbs: • *give* = *given* • *make* = _____, • *bring* = _____,

     • *help* = _____, • *take* = _____, • *open* = _____.

J. A verb in the passive is _____ _____ _____ _____ _____ _____.

K. All our soccer games were played on the weekend (by our team). (_____)

L. My mother painted this picture. = _____.

M. This hotel was built by a famous company.

N. Ken pays the rent every month. = _____.

Directions

Read these directions and questions <u>about the worksheet below</u> to your partners.

2. In Sentence A, write the word "active" in the blank.

5. In Sentence B, write the word "passive" in the blank.

8. Look at Sentence E. Write it in passive form in Sentence F.

11. In I, write the past participles for each of these verbs.

14. In Sentence K, write the letters "pp" above the past participle.

17. In your new Sentence L, write the word "be" above the auxiliary *be* and "pp" above the past participle.

20. In your new Sentence N, write the word "be" above the auxiliary *be* and "pp" above the past participle.

Passive Voice Worksheet

A. My brother helped me. (_____)

B. I was helped by my brother. (_____)

C. His girlfriend made him this sweater. (_____)

D. _____ was made by _____. (_____)

E. Those boys broke the window. (active)

F. The window _____ _____ by those boys. (passive)

G. Passive verb uses auxiliary *be* + _____ _____.

H. Auxiliary **be** includes *is*, _____, _____, *were*, _____ _____.

I. Past participles of verbs: • *give = given* • *make =* _____, • *bring =* _____,

   • *help =* _____, • *take =* _____, • *open =* _____.

J. A verb in the passive is _____ _____ _____ _____ _____ _____.

K. All our soccer games were played on the weekend (by our team). (_____)

L. My mother painted this picture. = _____.

M. This hotel was built by a famous company.

N. Ken pays the rent every month. = _____.

Directions

Read these directions and questions <u>about the worksheet below</u> to your partners.

3. In Sentence B, write S above the subject, AV above the auxiliary verb and V above the verb.

6. Is Sentence C active or passive? Write it in the blank.

9. I'll dictate G. Fill in the blanks with this: "The passive verb uses auxiliary *be* and the past participle."

12. I'll dictate J. Fill in the blanks with this: "A verb in the passive is often followed with a *by* phrase." (This is because the action is done *by* someone or *by* something.)

15. In Sentence K, notice the words "by our team." These words are optional. Write "optional" in the blank.

18. In Sentence M, write the word "be" above the auxiliary *be* and "pp" above the past participle.

Passive Voice Worksheet

A. My brother helped me. (_____)

B. I was helped by my brother. (_____)

C. His girlfriend made him this sweater. (_____)

D. _____ was made by _____. (_____)

E. Those boys broke the window. (active)

F. The window _____ _____ by those boys. (passive)

G. Passive verb uses auxiliary *be* + _____ _____.

H. Auxiliary **be** includes *is*, _____, _____, *were*, _____ _____.

I. Past participles of verbs: • *give* = *given*   • *make* = _____, • *bring* = _____,
    • *help* = _____,   • *take* = _____,   • *open* = _____.

J. A verb in the passive is _____ _____ _____ _____ _____ _____.

K. All our soccer games were played on the weekend (by our team). (_____)

L. My mother painted this picture. = _____.

M. This hotel was built by a famous company.

N. Ken pays the rent every month. = _____.

Unit 29
Passive Voice

Passive Voice
(Auxiliary **be** + <u>past participle</u> (by someone)

- The child **was** <u>found</u> by the police.
- The child **was** <u>found</u>. (*optional:* "by the police")

Exercise 1: Write the **past participles** for each of these verbs.

1. break: ___*broken*___   6. do: _____   11. hit: _____
2. build: _____   7. find _____   13. keep: _____
3. buy: _____   8. give: _____   14. leave: _____
4. catch: _____   9. hear: _____   15. lose: _____
5. choose: _____   10. hide: _____   16. send: _____

Exercise 2:

❶. Write **be** above the auxiliary *be*.
❷. Write **pp** above the past participle.

         be **pp**
1. All her money was spent on new CDs.

2. Tim's new car is kept in his garage.

3. We will be picked up by the hotel van at noon.

4. The leaders were chosen by the voters.

Exercise 3:

❶. Write **Passive** next to the sentences that are in the passive voice.
❷. Write **Active** next to the ones that are in the active voice.

_____ 1. They had their wedding on an island.

_____ 2. The corn was grown by my grandfather.

_____ 3. All his work was done before he went home.

_____ 4. They received a prize for their victory.

_____ 5. The news about the robbery was announced on the radio.

Common mistake: Writing sentences that look like they are passive.

(mistake) Schools <u>are start</u> at 7:30.
(correct) Schools <u>start</u> at 7:30.

(mistake) Parents <u>are worry</u> that their children will fail.
(correct) Parents <u>worry</u> that their children will fail.

(mistake) I <u>was stolen</u> my watch. *(There can be no "by someone" in this sentence.)*
(correct) My watch was stolen.
(correct) Someone <u>stole</u> my watch.

Exercise 4:

❶. Write **Right** if the verbs in the sentences are correct. There are four correct ones.
❷. Write **Wrong** if the verbs in the sentences are not correct.
❸. If the verbs are not correct, change them.

Wrong   1. Jim was disappointed because the car was <u>~~sell~~</u> *sold* already.

_____ 2. The dishes <u>were washed</u> and <u>put</u> away before I got home.

_____ 3. The police <u>will give</u> you a ticket if you drive too fast.

_____ 4. They <u>are work</u> hard even when they are tired.

_____ 5. My sister <u>was broken</u> her coffee cup.

_____ 6. My sister's cup <u>was broken</u>.

_____ 7. The presents <u>were hidden</u> by their parents.

_____ 8. The fish <u>will catch</u> tomorrow.

_____ 9. After 15 years, the brothers <u>were meet</u> at a family picnic.

_____10. I <u>was lost</u> my key, so I couldn't get in my house.

Unit 30

Sentences Starting with Dependent Clauses

Exercise 1:

❶. Choose six of the dependent clauses from the box below.

❷. Write sentences that start with the dependent clauses.

- Although Tom wanted to buy the car, **X**
- Because Sara was tired, __
- Until Don got his computer, __
- Since our school is famous for its great students, __
- Because my country has a (<u>cool climate / warm climate</u>), __
  (choose one)

- While the children were playing, __
- Before the boys went home, __
- Whenever I go there, __
- If I graduate from this school, __

---

1. *Although Tom wanted to buy the car, he didn't have enough money.*

2. _____

3. _____

4. _____

5. _____

6. _____

Exercise 2: Starting with independent clauses, write five sentences about your studies.

1. _____

2. _____

3. _____

4. _____

5. _____

Other books from Pro Lingua
AT THE INTERMEDIATE AND ADVANCED LEVELS

Also by David and Peggy Kehe

- **Conversation Strategies** — 24 structured pair activities for developing strategic conversation skills at the intermediate level. Students learn the words, phrases, and conventions used by native speakers in active, give-and-take, everyday conversation.

- **Discussion Strategies** — Carefully structured pair and small group work at the advanced-intermediate level. Excellent preparation for students who will participate in academic or professional work that requires effective participation in discussion and seminars.

Shenanigames — Grammar-focused, interactive ESL activities and games providing practice with a full range of grammar structures. Photocopyable.

Getting a Fix on Vocabulary — A student text and workbook that focuses on affixation — building words by adding prefixes and suffixes to a root.

Lexicarry — Pictures for Learning Languages the Active Way. Over 4500 everyday words and expressions in 192 contexts that make conversation and interactive learning easy. There is a special new section on proverbs and sayings. Lots of words, even for very advanced students. Additional material at www.Lexicarry.com.

Stranger in Town — A dramatic radio play in which the stranger moving to a small town is a metaphor for the process of cultural adjustment. Tapescript book and tape.

Nobel Prize Winners — 18 brief biographies for listening and/or reading. All the reading passages are also available as gapped exercises for reading or dictation. Text and three cassettes.

Write for You — A teacher resource book with copyable handouts. The focus is on creative activities that lead to effective writing by intermediate students who are intending to further their education.

Dictation and Discussion — Students start with the dictation of an interesting article which then becomes the basis for class discussion. There are four dictation formats, six topical areas: Cultural Trends, Money and Work, Holidays, Ethics, Health, and Fun (puzzles, games, jokes).

Pearls of Wisdom — At the heart of this integrated skills builder are twelve stories from Africa and the Caribbean, collected and told by Dr. Raouf Mama of Benin. Student text for reading/listening, workbook for discussion/vocabulary building, two cassettes.

Web Store: www.ProLinguaAssociates.com